COERCING VIRTUE

THE WORLDWIDE RULE OF JUDGES

ROBERT H. BORK

VINTAGE CANADA
A Division of Random House of Canada Limited

National Library of Canada Cataloguing in Publication Data

Bork, Robert H.
    Coercing virtue : the worldwide rule of judges

(The Barbara Frum lectureship)
ISBN 0-679-31093-2

1. Political questions and judicial power. 2. Judicial process. I. Title. II.
Series: The Barbara Frum lecture series.

K3367.B67 2002   347'.012   C00-932466-6

Text design: Valerie Applebee

Printed and bound in Canada

www.randomhouse.ca

2 4 6 8 9 7 5 3 1

*To my mother, Elizabeth K. Bork,
and to the memory of
my father, Harry P. Bork*

ACKNOWLEDGMENTS

As is usually the case, the efforts of a number of people go into the making of a book. Laura Hardy, my secretary, not only types, retypes, and proofreads drafts but handles the outside world in a way that makes writing possible. Not much would get done without her assistance.

Sarah Davies, executive editor at Random House Canada, has been a model of patience and accommodated my view that deadlines are infinitely flexible – almost. Rosemary Shipton proved to be an excellent and meticulous editor. Both of them were a pleasure to work with.

Evelyn Gordon rendered so much extremely valuable assistance on the chapter concerning Israel that she really should be listed as a co-author. She should not, however, be burdened with any mistakes and omissions that remain. *Azure* magazine, for which she frequently writes, contains a great deal of information about judicial activism in Israel in articles by Daniel Polisar, Evan Gahr, Hillel Neuer, and Mordechai Haller. Very useful commentary also appears in Jonathan Rosenbloom's articles in the *Jerusalem Post*.

John C. Yoo and Jack Goldsmith read and improved the chapter on international law. Christopher Manfredi and F. L. Morton provided assistance concerning Canadian judicial activism, and Manfredi vetted that chapter. The help of all four scholars was essential and much appreciated.

Daniel Troy once more read much of the manuscript and made very useful suggestions. A number of interns provided research and commentary. Christian Bonat undertook his assignments intelligently and assiduously, producing reams of material that contributed greatly to the final product. He has worked full time, researching and writing. Summer interns, whose tenures were necessarily brief, included Jared Hansen, Richard Barrett, and Adam Storch.

I am grateful once more to the American Enterprise Institute, which supported me in this endeavor. The views expressed here are my own and are not necessarily shared by AEI or by any of the people I have thanked.

INTRODUCTION

*I believe there are more instances of the abridgment
of the freedom of the people by gradual and silent
encroachments of those in power than by violent
and sudden usurpation.*

James Madison

*The death of democracy is not likely to be an
assassination from ambush. It will be a slow extinction
from apathy, indifference, and undernourishment.*

Robert Maynard Hutchins

The nations of the West have long been afraid of catching the "American disease" – the seizure by judges of authority properly belonging to the people and their elected representatives. Those nations are learning, perhaps too late, that this imperialism is not an American disease; it is a judicial disease, one that knows no boundaries. The malady appears wherever judges have been given or have been able to appropriate the power to override the decisions of other branches of government – the power of judicial review. That is why we see in virtually all Westernized nations dramatic and unplanned changes in governments and in cultures.

It is apparent even to a casual observer that, everywhere, democracy and indigenous moral traditions are in retreat. Even as more nations adopt democratic forms of government, the reforms are undermined by other internal developments. This is particularly noticeable in older, advanced democracies. Increasingly, the power of the people of Western nations to govern themselves is diluted, and their ability to choose the moral environment in which they live is steadily diminished.

It would be a mistake to attribute all these changes to the courts. There are many forces driving this development – the rise of relatively unaccountable and powerful bureaucracies, the decline of belief in authoritative religions, the acceptance of an ethos of extreme individual autonomy, the influence of the mass media, the explosion in size of the academic intellectual class, and more. This book, however, will concentrate on what seems to me the single most powerful influence aiding and abetting all other forces: the recent ascendancy almost everywhere of activist, ambitious, and imperialistic judiciaries. Oddly enough, the role of the courts in displacing self-government and forcing new moralities has not triggered a popular backlash. Courts have been and remain far more esteemed than the democratic institutions of government, even though the courts systematically frustrate the popular will as expressed in laws made by elected representatives.

Judicial activism results from the enlistment of judges on one side of the culture war in every Western nation. Despite denials by some that any such conflict exists, the culture war is an obtrusive fact. It is a struggle between the cultural or liberal left and the great mass of the citizenry who, left to their own devices, tend to be traditionalists. The courts are enacting the agenda of the cultural left. There is a certain embarrassment in choosing a name for this group. We often call its members the "intellectual class," the "intelligentsia," the "elite," the "knowledge class," or, dismissively, the "chattering class." Most of these names have the unfortunate connotation of superiority to the general public. That implication is not justified and is certainly not intended here. Individual members of the intellectual class are not necessarily, or even commonly, adept at intellectual work. Rather, their defining characteristic is that they traffic, at wholesale or retail, in ideas, words, or images and have meager or no practical experience of the subjects on which they expound. Intellectuals are, as Friedrick Hayek put it, "secondhand dealers in ideas." Their function is "neither that of the original thinker nor that of the scholar or

expert in a particular field of thought. The typical intellectual need be neither: he need not possess special
knowledge of anything in particular, nor need he even be
particularly intelligent, to perform his role as intermedi-
ary in the spreading of ideas." I will sometimes refer to
these faux intellectuals as the "New Class," a term that
suggests a common class outlook and indicates the
group's relatively recent rise to power and influence.

The New Class consists of print and electronic journalists; academics at all levels; denizens of Hollywood;
mainline clergy and church bureaucracies; personnel of
museums, galleries, and philanthropic foundations; radical
environmentalists; and activist groups for a multiplicity of
single causes. These are clusters of like-minded folk and
they have little knowledge or appreciation of people not
like themselves. As G.K. Chesterton wrote:

> In all extensive and highly civilized societies
> groups come into existence founded upon what is
> called sympathy, and shut out the real world more
> sharply than the gates of a monastery.... [T]he
> men of a clique live together because they have the
> same kind of soul, and their narrowness is a nar-
> rowness of spiritual coherence and contentment,
> like that which exists in hell.

Without presuming to know the spiritual condition that
prevails in hell – which, in Chesterton's version, sounds
more comfortable than the usual descriptions of the place
and, in fact, remarkably like a faculty lounge – it is

certainly true that the members of the New Class are generally smug and content in their liberal outlook.

It may not be immediately obvious why the New Class should be overwhelmingly liberal in outlook. Perhaps the best explanation is one offered a long time ago by Max Weber. Intellectuals characteristically display a strong desire for meaning in life, and, for them, meaning requires transcendent principles and universalistic ideals. These qualities were once conferred by religion, but, religion no longer being an option for intellectuals, the only alternative is the utopian outlook of the left. Once the hard-core varieties of the left were put out of favor by World War II and the Cold War, the intelligentsia turned to the softer and eclectic socialism of modern liberalism. The various attitudes expressed in modern liberalism add up to an overarching sentiment that must, for the time being, make do for a more explicit utopian vision. Socialism is, of course, the only available secular utopian vision of our time.

As a political and cultural philosophy or impulse, conservatism or traditionalism offers no comparable transcendentalism, no prospect of utopia. Conservatism is infrequently an option for the intelligentsia; the New Class despises the few conservatives to be found in its ranks more than it does those whom it regards as the retrograde "unwashed" – the general public. Conservative pragmatism, especially its concern with particularity – respect for difference, circumstance, tradition, history, and the irreducible complexity of human beings and human societies – does not qualify as a universal principle, but competes with and holds absurd the idea of a utopia achievable in this world.

What these rival philosophies all add up to is, in the familiar phrase, a revolution or a war within the culture. As Roger Kimball wrote: "A cultural revolution, whatever the political ambitions of its architects, results first of all in a metamorphosis in values and the conduct of life." In its overt form, the culture war is fought by "elites," the large majority of them liberal. The opposing sides in this revolutionary war are described by James Davison Hunter:

> One moral vision is predicated upon the assurance that the achievements and traditions of the past should serve as the foundation of communal life and guide us in negotiating today's and tomorrow's challenges. Though often tinged with nostalgia, this vision is misunderstood by those who label it as reactionary. In fact, this vision is neither regressive nor static, but rather is both syncretic and dynamic. Nevertheless, the order of life sustained by this vision does seek deliberate continuity with the guiding principles inherited from the past. The goal of this vision is the reinvigoration and realization in our society of what traditionalists consider to be the noblest ideals and achievements of civilization.

According to Hunter:

> Against this traditionalism is a moral vision that is ambivalent about the legacy of the past – it regards

the past in part as a curiosity, in part an irrelevance, in part a useful point of reference, and in part a source of oppression.... Its aim is the further emancipation of the human spirit.

Hunter does not adequately describe the dynamism and intolerance of the liberal or socialist side of the struggle. The "further emancipation of the human spirit" is, in fact, code for a cultural revolution that changes our values.

The culture war, as already suggested, is also a class war. Peter Berger wrote that "the 'carriers'... of the cultural radicalism of the late 1960s have had a very specific social character in all Western countries – overwhelmingly belonging to an upper middle class with higher education." Initiated by upper-middle-class students, the turmoil of the 1960s centered in the most prestigious universities, where the allegedly rigid and oppressive Establishment, having the same social characteristics and, in diluted form, many of the same values as the rioting students, immediately went limp. On graduation, the radical students went where they could best influence ideas and undercut traditional values. Thirty years on, they control the left wing of American politics and almost all the nation's cultural institutions, including, still, the universities. Other Western nations have traveled much the same route.

The values of the New Class differ sharply from traditional values. Berger notes that "attitudes toward religion and the place of religion in society are a key determinant of who stands where in the conflict. Opposing norms span personal morality (sexual behavior and abortion) and the legitimacy of the state (religious symbols in public places, prayer in public schools)." "There is," he said, "one feature of [normative conflicts] that reappears cross-nationally – a highly secularized cultural elite with a general population that continues to be deeply religious." Just how genuinely religious those populations are may be debatable, but it is true that, almost everywhere, the public views religion very favorably, even when regarding it as a form of therapy and being selective about obedience to its doctrines and obligations. There is less ambiguity about the cultural elites: they are so thoroughly secularized that, in varying degrees, they not only reject personal belief but maintain an active hostility to religion and religious institutions.

These issues are far from the only ones around which the culture war rages. There are, for example, such hotly contested topics as abortion, the definition of family, the teaching of values in public schools, the state monopoly of primary and secondary education, the relevance of the European heritage in increasingly multicultural societies, funding for the arts and the purpose of art itself, homosexual rights, patriotism, "social justice," welfare, gender, and the never-ending subjects of race and ethnicity.

The New Class's problem in most nations is that its attitudes command only a political minority. It is able to exercise influence in many ways, but, when cultural and social issues become sufficiently clear, the intellectual class loses elections. It is, therefore, essential that the cultural left find a way to avoid the verdict of the ballot box. Constitutional courts provide the necessary means to outflank majorities and nullify their votes. The judiciary is the liberals' weapon of choice. Democracy and the rule of law are undermined while the culture is altered in ways the electorate would never choose.

It may be useful to view the culture war from an additional perspective. It is, at bottom, a question of allegiance to or rejection of the socialist ideal. Kenneth Minogue wrote that

> even socialists [have been convinced] – for the moment – that the economy must be left alone. What has not changed is the deep passion of reformers and idealists in our civilization to take over governments and use their authority to enforce a single right way of life. This impulse now focuses on social issues like sex, drugs, education, culture and other areas where a beneficent government aims to help what they patronizingly call "ordinary people."

These social or cultural issues are the area where constitutional courts regularly attack the institutions and laws of "ordinary people."

The socialist impulse remains the ruling passion of the New Class. What are the characteristics of an impulse toward socialism that manifest themselves in both the economic and the cultural aspects of life? A partial list would include a passion for a greater, though unspecified, degree of equality; a search for universal principles; radical autonomy for the individual, but only in a hierarchical and bourgeois culture (when that culture has been eroded and replaced, there will be little tolerance for individualism); radical feminism; and a rationalism that despises tradition and religion and supposes that man and society can be made anew by rational reflection. Rationalism accounts for much of the coercion, moral as well as legal, that modern liberalism employs. If reason seems to lead to certainties about the virtuous life, it follows that those who remain unconvinced or who resist are perverse, or worse, in their refusal to accept the truth and must, therefore, be forced to cease their resistance.

To these qualities might be added a softness of spirit, a desire to ensure that no one, other than intellectual enemies, suffer the least degree of discomfort. The socialist economic vision, after all, stressed the desirability of a world in which no one experiences anything less than a comfortable material life. The same attitude may extend to the cultural and psychic components of life. It is not entirely clear whether this view is an aspect of the socialist impulse or whether it is merely the inevitable attitude prevalent in an affluent, technologically advanced society in which comfort and convenience have become the primary goods. Whatever the explanation, an exaggerated solicitude for the feelings of people is to be found in the jurisprudence of activist courts. It is by no means an undifferentiated solicitude, however, and it contains a strong ideological component. The comfort of some often requires the discomfort of others, and the gavel falls in favor of those the New Class favors.

The discredited economic theory of socialism is

merely one manifestation of a strong preference for the universal over the particular, and the most universal and least individualistic social principle is equality. Economic inequality being beyond reach, the attack turns to "lifestyle" inequalities, to a demand that we cease judging people and their actions according to the traditional moral scale. Traditionalists denounce this approach as moral relativism, but it is not that at all. Cultural socialists have their own moralities, often enforced with a fierceness unknown to upholders of the old moralities. That fanaticism is manifest in what we call "political correctness." "Nonjudgmentalism" is the first step toward a harsh judgmentalism in the service of a different morality. The war is religious in the intensity of belief, particularly on the liberal side, and because it is about the definition of virtue, morality, and the proper way of living.

The demand for radical autonomy, of which radical feminism is a component, is often phrased as a struggle for human liberation. Kimball sums up the effects of the "spirit of liberation" that exploded in the 1960s. His description is bleak, but not, I think, exaggerated:

> That ideology has insinuated itself, disastrously, into the curricula of our schools and colleges; it has significantly altered the texture of sexual relations and family life; it has played havoc with the authority of churches and other repositories of moral wisdom; it has undermined the claims of civic virtue and our national self-understanding; it has degraded the media, the entertainment industry,

and popular culture; it has helped to subvert museums and other institutions entrusted with preserving and transmitting high culture. It has even, most poignantly, addled our hearts and innermost assumptions about what counts as the good life: it has perverted our dreams as much as it has prevented us from attaining them.

This list illustrates the tendency of autonomy and liberation to turn into uniformity and coercion once traditional or bourgeois values have been discredited and displaced. The rigid conformity of thought and speech now enforced in many colleges and universities is but a single example.

The one institution noticeably missing from Kimball's recital is law. In discussions of cultural warfare, law is usually overlooked. Perhaps that is because law is viewed as a separate discipline, its movements, disputes, and modes of reasoning peculiar to itself. This view is obviously inadequate. Law is a key element of every Western nation's culture, particularly as we turn more to litigation than to moral consensus as the means of social control. Law is also more crucial today because courts have become more overtly cultural and political as well as legal institutions. Courts have played major roles in most of the pathologies Kimball lists, both by breaking down the traditional legal barriers societies have erected against degeneracy and by offering moral lessons based on the emancipatory spirit. In a word, courts in general have enlisted on the liberal side of the culture war. They are infected, as is the New Class to which judges belong and to which they respond, with the socialist impulse.

Just as the war is now an international phenomenon, so is judicial activism. The two necessarily go together because the new morality is not to be found in the constitutions judges profess to be interpreting. They must, therefore, invent new meanings in order to carry out the New Class program.

What does it mean to call a judge "activist" and "imperialistic"? The terms are bandied about freely by politicians and members of the media in an unedifying cross fire of slogans that passes for public debate, by politicians and members of the media, so that it will be useful to give those terms more stable meanings. Activist judges are those who decide cases in ways that have no plausible connection to the law they purport to be applying or who stretch or even contradict the meaning of that law. They arrive at results by announcing principles that were never contemplated by those who wrote and voted for the law. The law in question is usually a constitution, perhaps because the language of a constitution tends to be general and, in any event, judicial overreaching is then virtually immune to correction by the legislature or by the public.

Though judges rule in the name of a constitution and their authority is accepted as legitimate only because they are regarded as the keepers of a sacred text in a civic religion, there is no guarantee that the results actually come from that constitution. As Bishop Hoadly said almost three centuries ago, "Whoever hath an absolute authority to interpret any written or spoken laws, it is he who is truly the lawgiver, to all intents and purposes, and not the person who first wrote or spoke them." Judges who are conscious of that fact can, of course, do their best to interpret the law as the original authors intended. They can be properly active in the enforcement of liberties confided to their care, but not activist in creating new and unwarranted rights and liberties in defiance of democratic authority. Judges are activist if they pursue an agenda that cannot be validated by any reasonable construction of a constitution. Self-denial is unattractive, and judges have manifold opportunities to surrender to the temptation to enact their own beliefs. Such performances do not accord with any known version of the rule of law, but are, instead, nothing more than politics masquerading as law. It is often easier to predict the outcome of a case by knowing the names of the judges than by knowing the applicable legal doctrine. The nations of the West are increasingly governed not by law or elected representatives, but by unelected, unrepresentative, unaccountable committees of lawyers applying no law other than their own will.

The question of why most judges impose New Class attitudes is simply answered. Those attitudes are congenial to them, and the adoption of such attitudes is important to their reputations. Judges passed through colleges and law schools are themselves certified members of the intelligentsia. The ideas and values of the New Class are part of the furniture of most judges' minds and seem self-evident. Beyond that, the prestige of a judge depends on being thought and spoken well of in universities, law schools, and the media, all bastions of the New Class.

Very liberal judges are routinely spoken of as "moderates," while judges who attempt to apply a law as it was originally understood are equally routinely called "conservative" or "right wing." Whether a judge deliberately caters to these organs of the New Class or is unconsciously conditioned by praise and criticism to behave in accordance with the class's tenets, the effect is to move him to the culture left. A byproduct of this shift is a decline in the quality of judicial opinions, a decline that occasionally results in incoherence. Judicial systems were typically not designed for cultural and political roles. In adopting them, judges not only exceed their authority but perform poorly, often simplemindedly. Their training lies in such mundane but essential skills as reading perceptively, thinking logically, and writing clearly about precedents, statutes, and constitutions, not in pondering philosophy and social justice. However inadequate the moral philosophizing of judges may be, in this new role courts still speak self-confidently and with ultimate authority.

As the culture war has become global, so has judicial activism. Everywhere judicial review has taken root, activist courts align themselves with and enforce New Class values, shifting the culture steadily to the left. As the battle crosses national boundaries, moreover, it becomes less a series of parallel wars and, at the level of legal intellectuals, increasingly a single struggle. This shift is occurring not only because of the creation of supranational courts but because judges on national courts have begun to confer with their foreign counterparts and to cite foreign constitutional decisions as guides to the interpretation of their own constitutions. One telling indication of the judicial activism and uniformity of outlook among judges is the fact that the legal interpretation of constitutions with very different texts and histories is giving way to common attitudes expressed in judicial rulings. Judicial imperialism is manifest everywhere, from the United States to Germany to Israel, from Scandinavia to Canada to Australia, and it is now the practice of international tribunals. The problem is not created simply by a few unfortunate judicial appointments, but by a deeper cause and one more difficult to combat – the transnational culture war.

A remarkable aspect of this development is the degree to which the general public is unaware that judges, as a group, hold and systematically advance values hostile to their own. The public does not realize that individual decisions they deplore are not mistakes, but aspects of an agenda, and that, together, they add up to a claim to legislate the moral environment of the society. Politicians try occasionally to make an issue of lawless judicial behavior, but the response by the electorate is tepid to nonexistent. The trend to transform political and moral questions into legal issues, and thereby transfer power from elected legislatures and executives to unaccountable courts, continues.

In many Western nations today democracy is regarded as inconceivable without judicial review, even though several of those nations were functioning democracies without such review in the recent past. Perhaps Nazi atrocities across Europe created a desire for additional safeguards, though it is unlikely that the Nazis would have been deterred in the slightest, at any stage, by rulings from constitutional courts. Equally important is the American example of judicial review, which is generally regarded abroad as an unqualified success. But perhaps the most powerful impetus is New Class recognition that an activist judiciary helps to achieve the ends that democratic branches of government would withhold. The universities and the mass media, therefore, glorify the activism of the courts.

It is a dismal reflection on our times that few people other than activist groups and cultural elites, who want more of the same, seem to be concerned about the gradual replacement of democracy by judicial rule. This takeover is not a minor matter of judicial philosophy, of interest only to the theoretically inclined. At stake are personal freedoms. The fundamental freedom recognized in democracies is the right of the people to govern themselves. Specified constitutional rights are meant to be exceptions, not the rule. When, in the name of a "right," a court strikes down the desire of the majority, expressed through laws, freedom is transferred from a larger to a smaller group, from a majority to a minority. When judges strike down a law on grounds not to be found in the constitution, we are all more free – free to act in ways that most of us had decided were unacceptable.

Activist courts accomplish their ends by a combination of coercion and moral persuasion. Courts inevitably assume the role of moral teachers. Normative values pronounced, even falsely, in the name of a constitution often come to be accepted by the public and are then reflected and intensified in legislatures, schools, and other

institutions. "An idea, adopted by a court," Edward H.
Levi observed, "is in a superior position to influence conduct and opinion in the community; judges, after all, are
rulers. And the adoption of an idea by a court reflects the
power structure in a community." The power structure
today is in the hands of the New Class. People who are
repeatedly told by the constitutional clerisy that the fundamental document on which their nation rests requires
tolerance of obscenity, sexual deviance, abortion on
demand, or the banishment of religion in public places,
all in the name of "rights" and the emancipation of the
human spirit, are likely to absorb the lesson as the only
outlook proper for a decent person.

The vocabulary of "rights" is, everywhere, the rhetoric by which judicial power advances. Rights are not only
universal but dynamic, while the pragmatic considerations that oppose their expansion are not. Rights talk is
inspiring; prudence talk is not. Particularities are usually
more difficult to defend than universals, so rights talk
continues to expand in common discourse, political plat-
itudes, and the rulings of the judiciary.

The tendency of many countries to turn to courts is
accelerated by the rapid diversification of the racial and
ethnic compositions of their populations. New self-pro-
claimed victim groups clamor for relief from majority
rule. No binding moral or social consensus remains.
Gertrude Himmelfarb finds it "ironic" that the idea of a
single community "persists in spite of the fragmentation
that has taken place in recent years as a result of multiculturalism, affirmative action, radical feminism, and the

conflicting imperatives of the race/class/gender schema. There is, in fact, little coherence or commonality left in the 'community' that is at the heart of communitarianism." Yet, as Lord Devlin put it, "What makes a society is a community of ideas, not political ideas alone but also ideas about the way its members should behave and govern their lives." When other forces lose their cohesive powers, it is inevitable that people will look to law as the last remaining universal bearer of values and the source of justice. This outcome may put more weight on law than it can bear, for, as Lord Devlin also said, "If the whole dead weight of sin were ever to be allowed to fall upon the law, it could not take the strain." So, too, if the whole dead weight of social incoherence is to fall upon the law, as it appears to be doing, the law may well collapse under the pressure. As law begins to fail, the response is to demand more law, and the preferred form, by intellectuals and victim groups alike, is a judge-invented and fragmenting constitutional law. Law thus perversely intensifies the strain it already bears.

Courts possess very potent powers, both coercive and moral. Although that power is asserted over an entire culture, it is not always dramatic because it proceeds incrementally, but, since the increments accumulate, it is all the more potent for that. What judges have wrought is a coup d'état – slow-moving and genteel – but a coup d'état nonetheless.

In an essay of this size it is not possible to discuss the constitutional laws of all nations in any great detail. I have chosen as representative examples the judicial trends in constitutional decisions in the United States, Canada, and Israel, as we will see in chapters 2, 3, and 4. The courts of these three nations run the gamut of judicial imperialism. European nations are discussed in chapter 5 as a group, insofar as they have surrendered their sovereignty in these matters to international tribunals. Those tribunals display the same activism as the national courts.

It is not to be expected that all courts will reach identical results. Given conflicting outcomes on particular issues, however, the courts of different nations display a tendency that is the same everywhere: the continuing usurpation by the courts of the authority lodged in democratic government, along with the movement of societies to the cultural left. These trends may in time be halted, but, at present, there is little evidence of any reversal.

1

UNITED STATES

*What secret knowledge, one must wonder, is breathed
into lawyers when they become Justices of this Court,
that enables them to discern that a practice which the
text of the Constitution does not clearly proscribe, and
which our people have regarded as constitutional for
200 years, is in fact unconstitutional? . . . Day by
day, case by case, [the Court] is busy designing a
Constitution for a country I do not recognize.*

Justice Antonin Scalia

Save America. Close Yale Law School.

Bumper sticker

Judicial review as practiced in the United States provides a case study of what other countries may expect,
and many are already experiencing, as they take up the
same form of constitutionalism. The lesson is not an
entirely happy one. Along with the undoubted successes
of judicial dominance has come a virulent judicial
activism that increasingly calls into question the authority of representative government and the vitality of traditional values as they evolve through nonjudicial
institutions, public and private. Instead, Americans are
force fed a new culture and new definitions of virtue, all
in the name of a Constitution that neither commands
nor permits such results. America is moving from the
rule of law to the rule of judges. Other countries that
adopt judicial review will know similar results.

The United States Supreme Court adopted a form of
judicial review more than two centuries ago and formal-
ized it eleven years later, in 1803, long before the courts
of any other nation. Exercised sparingly for several
decades, the Court's power to nullify the actions of the
political branches of government was then increasingly
deployed until, today, the exercise of that power has
become routine. One of America's boasts is that it has the
oldest Constitution in the world, while other nations
have found it necessary to frame one new version after
another. The boast is not entirely justified. The question
of amendments aside, the Constitution Americans live
under today has, both by force of circumstance and judicial activism, become something radically different in
many ways from the document that was drafted in

Philadelphia in 1787. Nevertheless, the United States's experience with judicial review is now internationally regarded as an almost unqualified success and a model for other democratic nations. The reality is both more complicated and less inspiring.

There is no doubt that judicial review has produced great benefits in the protection of essential freedoms. There is also, unfortunately, little doubt that the practice increasingly denies valuable freedoms that the Constitution was meant to protect. As the epigraph at the head of this chapter suggests, judicial dominance is exerted not only over the democratic branches of government but over the Constitution itself. The fundamental question for practitioners of the law has become not what the Constitution means – interpreted according to its text, history, and structure – but what judges have said and will say about it.

The epigraph accurately states one result of the New Class's march through the institutions of American culture – the capture of the Supreme Court of the United States by the New Class and its conversion, to a degree hitherto unprecedented, from a legal forum to a political and cultural tribunal enforcing the values of the liberal intelligentsia. Almost no one fails to realize the new and dominant role of the Court – although many New Class apologists insist, disingenuously, that the Court is now simply interpreting the Constitution. Both sides recognize, however, that the Court has far transcended any such modest and mundane role. As a predictable consequence, the Court's work is judged politically and the filling of vacancies on the retirement or death of Justices can set off major political battles. At such times, partisans on both sides anxiously anticipate possible departures from the Court, consider the composition of the Senate (which must confirm or reject the president's nominees), and estimate the financial reserves each side will be able to bring to the campaign.

That much is new, though activism itself is by no means entirely unprecedented. Though isolated, there have always been instances of willful distortions of the law. In fact, the first broad claim of judicial authority to nullify acts of the legislature came in an instance of judicial activism that is impressive even by today's standards. In *Marbury* v. *Madison* (1803), Marbury, who had been promised a patronage appointment as justice of the peace by the previous administration, challenged the new administration under President Thomas Jefferson when it failed to make the appointment. Marbury filed in the Supreme Court for an order (a mandamus) requiring James Madison, Jefferson's secretary of state, to deliver signed commissions for the position of justice of the peace. The Court was clearly without jurisdiction in this area and the case. Article III of the Constitution lists the categories of cases within the original jurisdiction of the Court. Marbury's case was not among them and should have been dismissed at once. Instead, Chief Justice John Marshall produced a lengthy, skillful, and intellectually dishonest opinion declaring, in effect, that Marbury was entitled to the appointment but that the Court could not force the president to make it. There can be no doubt that Marshall and the other members of the Court understood what they were doing. Marshall, an ardent Federalist, managed in one opinion to issue a ruling in a case without having jurisdiction, charge Thomas Jefferson's Republican administration with illegal conduct, misrepresent a statute as well as the common law, strike down as unconstitutional the distorted version of the statute he misrepresented for the occasion, and, finally, articulate a basis for a broad power of judicial review. Having accomplished all this, Marshall said he could not order relief, thus saving himself and the Court from the embarrassment of being defied by the defendant, James Madison.

This recital of multiple misbehaviors does not prove judicial review illegitimate, but the manner in which the Supreme Court established its authority was hardly propitious. Even so, the Marshall Court of 1803 could not have foreseen the uses to which the Court's authority was put in the twentieth century and, barring a miracle, will continue to be put in the twenty-first. Marshall justified judicial supremacy in the interpretation of the Constitution on the ground that the legislature must not be permitted to do what the Constitution forbids. The subsequent career of judicial review, however, demonstrates that courts, being uncheckable, freely do what the Constitution forbids while ordering others not to do what the Constitution allows.

The power of judicial review lay unexercised for fifty-four years until *Dred Scott* v. *Sandford* (1857), which was the worst constitutional decision of the nineteenth century – not merely in the immorality of its result and the speciousness of its reasoning, but because it is the true doctrinal ancestor of many modern constitutional follies. In this case the Court decided that the slave Dred Scott could not be declared free on the basis that he had been taken to Illinois, where slavery was forbidden by federal law. Chief Justice Roger Taney, writing for a majority of the Justices, could simply have dealt with the facts of the case and decided that Scott, as a slave, was not a citizen with standing to bring a lawsuit, but he went further and declared that the United States lacked the power to prohibit slavery in any state or territory or to permit a state to bar slavery in its own territory. That, he said, would deprive slave owners of their property without "due process of law." With this single sentence Taney converted a clause of the Fifth Amendment from a guarantee of a proper process in the application of law to a guarantee of a proper substance, or meaning (in the view of the Justices), of the law itself.

The Court would now be able to judge the constitutionality of law by deciding, without any criteria to structure the judgment, that the substance of what the law commanded was not "due." There could be no intellectual structure to substantive due process because its existence was unjustified, indeed contradicted, by the text, and the framers and ratifiers, of course, provided no legislative history for a concept they never intended. One might have expected this transparent sleight of hand from a Court trying to justify the unjustifiable. What could not have been foreseen was the scores of times the Court would use due process to substitute its law-making for that of the elected legislature.

If *Marbury* was motivated by Federalist politics and *Dred Scott* by sympathy with the slave states, the Court after the Civil War began to express the ideology of the rising business class. The most notorious example is *Lockner* v. *New York* (1905), which struck down a decision setting maximum work hours for bakers. Justice Peckham, writing for the majority, used the Due Process Clause of the Fourteenth Amendment to create a "liberty of contract," a concept found nowhere in the Constitution, to hold that any limitation on hours of work was unreasonable. Statutes of this type, he wrote, were "mere meddlesome interferences with the rights of the individual." Three of the Court dissenters even agreed that there was a liberty of contract. This freehand approach to constitutional argument was to have results that Peckham, let alone Marshall and Taney, would have abhorred. In the wake of the Great Depression, the next stage in the Court's ideological journey was the enforcement of New Class values, rather than those of the business class.

The one thing that stood in the way of a full-blown activism was the Court's fear of overreaching and a consequent political backlash. That fear must have seemed well founded after President Franklin Roosevelt, frustrated by the invalidation of much of the economic regulation of his New Deal, attempted to "pack" the Court by seeking legislation enabling him to appoint an additional Justice for every Justice who reached the age of seventy and did not retire. Six Justices were then over seventy. It soon became apparent, however, that a conservative activist Court was vulnerable in ways that a liberal activist

Court was not. The Court regained its confidence and the activist enterprise went into high gear after the decision in *Brown* v. *Board of Education* (1954). I have argued elsewhere that *Brown's* desegregation of public schools can find support in the Constitution, but, as demonstrated by the woefully inadequate opinion it issued, the Court did not think so. Yet, despite its belief that the decision had no real grounding in the Constitution, the Court saw that it could make a highly controversial decision stick, even over powerful opposition. Activism was safe, it believed, and the wraps were off.

What is this New Class agenda advanced by the Court?

The First Amendment: Speech and Religion
Perhaps no provisions of the Constitution are more central to American democracy and culture than those of the First Amendment's guarantee of speech and religious freedom:

> Congress shall make no law respecting an establishment of religion, or prohibiting the free exercise thereof; or abridging the freedom of speech, or of the press, or the right of the people peaceably to assemble, and to petition the Government for redress of grievances.[1]

---

[1]   *"Congress" has long since been interpreted to mean any arm of any government – national, state, or local.*

The First Amendment is pivotal. Nothing reveals more clearly the contest of views concerning the proper relationship between the individual and society. Equally clear, in the Court's recent deformation and reversal of the meaning of that amendment, is the rise to dominance of the New Class. Harry Kalven was correct in saying that freedom of speech is so close to the heart of democracy that, if we lack an appropriate theory of the First Amendment, we really do not understand the society in which we live. I would add that if we lack an appropriate theory of the Religion Clauses of the First Amendment, we do not understand the culture that religion in large measure formed nor the erosion of cultural virtues that the Court's new-found hostility to religion has abetted.

The Court had little occasion to consider First Amendment speech claims until the early years of the twentieth century; it did so particularly in prosecutions arising out of the First World War and what has become known as the Red Scare. Today, those cases are remembered less for the majority opinions than for the dissents by Justices Holmes and Brandeis that contained the seeds of doctrine that came to fruition in later years and are with us yet. I have expressed my doubts about those dissents elsewhere, but here I want to note that the assumption of complete human rationality made its debut in Holmes's dissent in *Abrams* v. *United States* (1919). The defendants were convicted for circulating pamphlets construed as harmful to the war effort. Holmes would have set aside the convictions on statutory grounds, which would have been entirely proper, but then proceeded in his glittering prose to introduce into the First Amendment an unfortunate assumption of rationalism:

> [W]hen men have realized that time has upset many fighting faiths, they may come to believe even more than they believe the very foundations of their own conduct that the ultimate good desired is better reached by free trade in ideas – that the test of truth is the power of thought to get itself accepted in the competition of the market.

This is a distinctly odd passage since Holmes, again in dissent, said elsewhere that the only meaning of the First Amendment was that the dominant force in the society must have its way, even though that might prove to be the dictatorship of the proletariat – hence the only meaning of the First Amendment is to permit the victory of a fighting faith over the free trade in ideas. That anomaly aside, underlying his argument that the test of truth is acceptance of an idea in the competitive market is the assumption that, in a future short enough to be worth waiting for, men will be rational actors. Since that is obviously not true, the metaphor can be fatally misleading. An economic market imposes a discipline that the marketplace of ideas does not. A producer of shoddy goods will soon find that consumers will turn elsewhere. A producer of shoddy ideas may be able to sell them indefinitely, as Nazism and communism demonstrate. Holmes certainly knew from history that horrible ideas were often accepted in the market. His own experience as a soldier demonstrated that, when ideas differ sharply enough, the "truth" of one or the other is not settled in the market but in the slaughter of the battlefield. Nevertheless, the compelling quality of his prose and the attractiveness to intellectuals of the notion of the ultimate supremacy of good ideas served, down to our own day, to make his extremely dubious version of appropriate constitutional policy the dominant one. A counterfactual rationalism has become a central tenet of the law of freedom of speech.

The core value of the First Amendment's Speech Clause is the protection of political speech, speech that informs and guides the political process essential to a republican form of government. Until recent years, the amendment was not understood to have anything to do with topics such as pornography and very little to do with subversive advocacy of revolutionary violence and law breaking. But now the First Amendment, as interpreted by Court majorities, has gone soft at its center while it becomes increasingly severe at its fringes.

The Speech Clause began to go soft with the 1976 decision in *Buckley* v. *Valeo* (1976). The Supreme Court upheld portions of the *Federal Election Campaign Act* limiting individual contributions to political candidates to quite small amounts, but held invalid restrictions on political expenditures. Though the statute was presented as an anti-corruption measure, its real effect was to limit and distort political speech. Had the Court-approved limits been in place in 1968, for instance, Eugene McCarthy's challenge to President Lyndon Johnson in the New Hampshire primary, a contest that persuaded the president not to seek re-election, could not have been mounted. McCarthy's campaign depended on very large individual contributions; he could not, in the time available, have raised the necessary funds from tens of thousands of small contributors.

Limiting contributions inhibits political speech in two ways. First, candidates are forced to spend large amounts of time raising money in small amounts – time they would otherwise devote to campaigning. Second, contributors make it possible for candidates to advance the contributors' views. The Court held that restrictions on contributions were valid because of the fear of corruption, or even the appearance of corruption. These concerns, however, could have been dealt with by public disclosure requirements.

The Federal Election Campaign Act and the decision in *Buckley* v. *Valeo*, moreover, have shifted political power in America toward those with the leisure to engage in political activity – toward students, toward labor unions with members willing to engage in door-to-door campaigning and to run telephone banks, toward journalists and those with free access to the media, toward candidates with great personal wealth they are free to spend, and toward incumbents who have provided themselves with a variety of political resources at public expense. Many of these shifts in power were planned intentionally by the groups favored, and most of them favor the New Class's liberal agenda.

Matters have not improved since 1976. In *Nixon* v. *Shrink Missouri Government PAC* (2000), the Court upheld a state law imposing even more drastic limitations on political contributions, in part to "democratize" political power and in part because, as Justice Stevens's concurrence put it, "Money is property; it is not speech." The first rationale is a perversion of the First Amendment. If democratization or equalization of speech were a valid reason, the Court should uphold a requirement that networks and newspapers employ equal numbers of liberal and conservative commentators. As to the second rationale, it would justify a ban on an owner's donation of his auditorium for a campaign rally or a homeowner's use of his living room for a political meeting. It might equally be said that telecasting equipment is property and not speech, but it is property without which political speech in a mass democracy would be utterly ineffective. It is difficult to see in *Shrink* anything other than what the dissenters said it was — a substantial suppression of political speech. The Court's disrespect for the central concern of the First Amendment bodes ill for freedom of political speech as new restrictions on campaign financing are proposed.

Any version of the First Amendment not built on the political speech core and confined by it, if not to it, will prove intellectually incoherent and will leave judges free to legislate as they will. Both of these unfortunate results stem from the weakening of the amendment's political core. They may also be seen in what the Supreme Court has made of the law relating to subversive speech and to pornography and obscenity.

The Court displays an extraordinary concern, indeed solicitude, for the well-being and vigor of subversive advocacy, whether it be American Nazis marching through a neighborhood having a substantial number of Holocaust survivors or speech urging the violation of law in the service of one or another cause. The willingness to protect such speech, though it is of no social or political value in a nation where elections are free, follows from Holmes's metaphor of open competition in the marketplace. This line of cases culminated in *Brandenburg* v. *Ohio* (1969), which laid down the rule that the Speech Clause does "not permit a State to forbid or proscribe advocacy of the use of force or of law violation except where such advocacy is directed to inciting or producing imminent lawless action and is likely to incite or produce such action." That extraordinary ruling replaced older law that saw little, if any, social value in the advocacy of forcible overthrow or law violation but did give weight to its dangers, even if the violence or law violation was not "imminent." *Brandenburg* would allow demagoguery to bring its audience to a boiling point and permit intervention by the state only when the last in a series of incitements was likely to produce action. That prescription will often be unworkable and, in any event, the conclusion makes little sense in a democracy where speech is directed to governing, not to the self-fulfillment of the demagogue or to minority violence.

A parallel development occurred in the alteration of the law relating to pornographic or obscene expression. This area is the one in which the Supreme Court's capture by the philosophy of radical individualism is perhaps most blatant. For two centuries, in fact ever since the establishment of the first colonies, Americans suppressed such expression. As late as 1942 a unanimous Court could say in *Chaplinsky* v. *New Hampshire* that prohibiting "the lewd and obscene, the profane, the libelous, and the insulting or 'fighting' words" had "never been thought to raise any Constitutional problem" because "such utterances are no essential part of any exposition of ideas, and are of such slight social value as a step to truth that any benefit that may be derived from them is clearly outweighed by the social interest in order and morality." Order and morality? In the culture created by modern liberalism, the words sound quaint, if not benighted and repressive.

The *Zeitgeist* mutated so rapidly that, in 1973, when a bare five-Justice majority upheld minor (and, as it proved, utterly ineffective) restraints on pornography in *Miller* v. *California*, there was a great outcry about censorship. Communities now find it impossible to control the torrent of pornography loosed upon them. Juries can no longer agree, as *Miller* requires, that any depiction of sexual conduct is "patently offensive" or that "the work, taken as a whole, lacks serious literary, artistic, political, or scientific value." And there is always a clutch of professors at hand to testify that the purest pornography is actually a profound parable about the horrors of capitalism or the repressiveness of the bourgeois state, or that, in any event, the photography or the prose has artistic value.

The Court has proved almost equally unable to cope with the problem of obscene speech. *Cohen* v. *California* (1971) threw First Amendment protection around a man who wore into a courthouse a jacket suggesting, with a

short Anglo-Saxon verb, that the reader perform a sexual
act of extreme anatomical implausibility with the
Selective Service System. Justice Harlan, writing for the
majority, relied on both the dangers of the slippery slope
and moral relativism. He said "the principle contended
for by the State seems inherently boundless. How is one
to distinguish this from any other offensive word?" He
might as well have said that, in tort law, the negligence
standard is inherently boundless: How is one to distinguish the reckless driver from the safe one? The answer in
both cases is the common sense of the community.
Almost all judgments in law are matters of degree, as, to
take another example, in distinguishing between libel and
fair comment. Harlan's other reason was a classic of moral
relativism: "One man's vulgarity," he said, "is another's
lyric." On that ground, it is impossible to see how law on
any subject can be allowed to exist if any citizen disagrees
with it. One man's armed robbery is, after all, another's
just redistribution of wealth.

The First Amendment does not enforce virtue, but the
Court should not misuse the guarantee to outlaw the
legitimate efforts of communities to slow the erosion of
moral standards, to safeguard the aesthetic environment,
and to set minimal standards for the decency of public discourse. If the First Amendment were interpreted, as it was
for most of our history, to permit such efforts, nothing of
any worth would be lost and much would be gained.

The inversion of the Speech Clause so that pornography and calls for violence and law violation are better
protected than political speech is a continuation of the

Court's transformation of the clause from an indispensable element of democratic government to a guarantee of individual self-gratification and diminished popular engagement in politics. This trend, too, is congenial to the scale of values advanced by the New Class.

Much the same may be said of the Court's interpretation of the Religion clauses of the First Amendment. The liberal intelligentsia is overwhelmingly secular and fearful of religion; hence its incessant harping on the dangers posed by the "religious right." That ominous phrase is intended to suggest that Americans who are conservative and religious are a threat to the Republic, for they are probably intending to establish a theocracy and to institute an ecumenical version of the Inquisition. (Exasperated, a friend suggested that the press should begin referring to the "pagan left.") It is certainly true, however, that the liberal intelligentsia's antagonism to religion is now a prominent feature of American jurisprudence. The Court moved rather suddenly from tolerance of religion and religious expression to fierce hostility. Though not the first manifestation, one case illustrates the place of religion on the Court's scale of values. Major philosophical shifts in the law sometimes occur through what may seem to laymen mere tinkerings with technical doctrine. The judiciary's power to marginalize religion in public life was vastly increased through a change in the law of what lawyers call "standing," which withholds the power to litigate from persons claiming only a generalized or ideological interest in an issue. Some direct impact on the plaintiff, such as the loss of money or liberty, is required. But in 1968, in *Flast* v. *Cohen*, the Supreme Court created the entirely novel rule that taxpayers can sue under the Establishment Clause to prohibit federal expenditures aiding religious schools. The Court refused to allow similar suits to be brought under other parts of the Constitution. Thus, every single provision of the Constitution, from Article I, section 1, to the Twenty-seventh Amendment, except one, is immune from taxpayer or citizen enforcement – and that exception is the one used to attack public manifestations of religion.

Now we are treated to the preposterous spectacle of lawsuits by persons whose only complaint is that they are "offended" by seeing a religious symbol, such as a creche or a menorah, on public property during a holiday season or even by the sight of the Ten Commandments on a plaque on a high school wall. Apparently those who do not like religion are exquisitely sensitive to the pain of being reminded of it, but the religious are assumed to have no right to such feelings about the banishment of religion from the public arena.

The distance between the Court's position on religion and the framers' and ratifiers' understanding of the First Amendment was revealed, though not for the first time, in *Lemon* v. *Kurtzman* (1971). The case created a three-part test which, if applied consistently, would erase all hints of religion in any public context. In order to survive judicial scrutiny a statute or practice must have a secular legislative purpose; its principal or primary effect must be one that neither advances nor inhibits religion; and it must not foster an excessive government entanglement with religion. Few statutes or governmental practices that brush anywhere in the vicinity of religion can pass all those tests.

Yet the Supreme Court narrowly approved Nebraska's employment of a chaplain for its legislature in *Marsh* v. *Chambers* (1983). Though the dissent correctly pointed out that the *Lemon* test was violated, as it was in each of its three criteria, the majority relied on the fact that employing chaplains to open legislative sessions with prayers conformed to historic precedent: not only did the Continental Congress employ a chaplain but so did both houses of the first Congress, which also proposed the First Amendment. That same Congress also provided paid chaplains for the Army and the Navy. The Court often pays little attention to the historic meaning of the Constitution, but it would be particularly egregious to hold that those who sent the amendment to the states for ratification intended to prohibit what they had just done themselves. That *Lemon* fails when specific historical evidence is available necessarily means that, in cases where specific history is not discoverable, *Lemon* destroys laws and practices that were meant to be allowable.

There is no lack of other evidence to show that no absolute barrier to any interaction between government and religion was intended. From the beginning of the Republic, Congress called upon presidents to issue Thanksgiving Day proclamations in the name of God. All the presidents complied, with the sole exception of Jefferson, who thought such proclamations at odds with the principle of the Establishment Clause. Jefferson's tossed-off metaphor in a letter about the "wall" between church and state has become the modern law, despite the fact that it was idiosyncratic and not at all what Congress and the ratifying states understood themselves to be saying. The first Congress readopted the Northwest Ordinance, initially passed by the Continental Congress, which stated that "religion, morality, and knowledge, being necessary to good government and the happiness of mankind, schools and the means of learning shall forever be encouraged." The ordinance required that specified amounts of land be set aside for churches.

Yet in *Lee* v. *Weisman* (1992) a six-Justice majority held that a short, bland, nonsectarian prayer at a public school commencement amounted to an establishment of religion. The Court saw government interference with religion in the very fact that the school principal asked the rabbi to offer a nonsectarian prayer. Coercion of Deborah Weisman was detected in the possibility that she might feel "peer pressure" to stand or at least to maintain respectful silence during the prayer. She would, of course, have had no constitutional case had the commencement speaker read from the Communist Manifesto or *Mein Kampf* and both peer pressure and school authorities required her to maintain a "respectful silence." Only religion is beyond the judge-erected pale. In this way a long tradition across the entire nation of prayer at public school graduation ceremonies came to an end.

One more example will suffice. In *Santa Fe Independent School Dist.* v. *Doe* (2000) the school district arranged student elections to determine whether invocations should be delivered before high school football games and, if so, to select the students to deliver them. The student chosen could make a statement or read a nonsectarian, nonprose-lytizing prayer. The Supreme Court majority held that "school sponsorship of a religious message is impermissi-ble because it sends the ancillary message to members of the audience who are nonadherents 'that they are out-siders, not full members of the political community, and an accompanying message to adherents that they are insiders, favored members of the political community.'" The non-adherent was put to "the choice between whether to attend these games or to risk facing a personally offensive religious ritual." The incredibly thin skin of nonadherents is constitutional dogma. The Court repeatedly referred to the elections as "majoritarian," as though that made them all the more threatening. The opinion is remarkable for a tone that "bristles with hostility to all things religious in public life," Chief Justice Rehnquist noted in dissent. The majority opinion, it might be said, also bristles with hostil-ity to majoritarian (i.e., democratic) processes. Still more remarkable, and sadly ironic, is the majority's statement that "one of the purposes served by the Establishment Clause is to remove debate over this kind of issue from govern-mental supervision or control." That is precisely what the decision does not do. The Court's pronounced antireli-gious animus, displayed in decades of decisions, has itself produced angry debate that is under the control of the Supreme Court, a branch of government.

At some point, parody is the only appropriate

response. Nude dancing is entitled to considerable protection as "expressive" behavior, according to *Erie* v. *Pap's A.M.* (2000). Theodore Olson, a leading Supreme Court advocate and now solicitor general of the United States, was prompted to suggest that high school students should dance nude before football games because naked dancing is preferred to prayer as a form of expression. He might have noted, of course, that nudity must not be achieved through the Dance of the Seven Veils because that has biblical connotations!

Lower courts have found a forbidden "establishment of religion" in the most innocuous practices: a high school football team praying before a game that nobody be injured; a local ordinance forbidding the sale of nonkosher foods as kosher; a small child trying to read a child's version of a religious story when told that each student must read a favorite story before the class; a teacher reading the Bible silently for his own purposes during a reading period because students, who were not shown to know what the teacher was reading, might, if they found out, be influenced by his choice of reading material. The Court's Establishment Clause decisions show the same devotion to radical individual autonomy as do the speech cases. The words "Congress shall make no law respecting an establishment of religion" might have been read, as common understanding would suggest, merely to preclude government recognition of an official church or to prohibit discriminatory aid to one or a few religions. No one reading the Establishment Clause when it was ratified in 1791 could have anticipated the unhistorical sweep it would develop under the sway of modern liberalism to produce, as Richard John Neuhaus put it, a "public square naked of religious symbol and substance."

The Court has brought law and religion into opposition. The results are damaging to both fields. All law rests upon choices guided by moral assumptions and beliefs. There is no reason to prohibit any conduct, except on the understanding that some moral good is thereby served. Though the proposition is certainly not undisputed, there is an excellent case to be made that religion, though not the original source of moral understanding, is an indispensable reinforcement of that understanding. It is surely significant that, as religious belief has declined, moral behavior has worsened as well. When law becomes antagonistic to religion, it undermines its own main support.

Christopher Lasch, who was by no means a conservative, asked: "What accounts for [our society's] wholesale defection from the standards of personal conduct – civility, industry, self-restraint – that were once considered indispensable to democracy?" He answered that a major reason is the "gradual decay of religion." Our liberal elites, whose "attitude to religion," Lasch said, "ranges from indifference to active hostility," have succeeded in removing religion from public recognition and debate. Indeed, it could be added that the Court has almost succeeded in establishing a new religion: secular humanism. That is what the intelligentsia want, it is what they are getting, and we may all be the worse for it.

Substantive Due Process

A more general judicial legislative power has been seized in the name of the Due Process Clause when no provision of the Constitution can, even with stretching or inversion, be found to apply. The Fifth and Fourteenth amendments require, respectively, due process by the federal government and the states: "No person shall...be deprived of life, liberty, or property, without due process of law." "Substantive due process" has been used over and over again since *Dred Scott* to strike down laws whose invalidation is not justified by any provision of the Constitution. John Hart Ely commented that "there is simply no avoiding the fact that the word that follows 'due' is 'process.'... '[S]ubstantive due process' is a contradiction in terms – sort of like 'green pastel redness.'" Once the clause was said to impose substantive requirements on statutes, there was, unfortunately, nothing to define or even to suggest what the substance of substantive due process might be. There was, and could be, only the impulse of the judge. Despite its fatal defects in law, logic, and history, however, the Court finds substantive due process too valuable a source of unconfined judicial law-making to be abandoned.

The clause's most notorious achievement in modern times was to serve as the textual peg for the Court-invented "right of privacy." *Griswold* v. *Connecticut* (1965) struck down a state law prohibiting the use of contraceptives. The law had been enforced, under the general accessory provision of the criminal code, only against birth control clinics that advertised contraception. The

Court's opinion argued that various guaranteed rights related to privacy – the rights of association, freedom from the quartering of soldiers in private homes, freedom from unreasonable searches and seizures, and so on – and that, from these rights, could be constructed a general, if undefined, right of privacy. Since the use of contraception was done in private, the Connecticut statute violated the Due Process Clause. A new right to be used as the Court desired had been invented. Using identical reasoning, Justice Brennan later said that the various freedoms guaranteed by the *Bill of Rights* were about dignity, so there is a general, again undefined, right to dignity. Since the death penalty subjects the condemned person to a loss of dignity, capital punishment, though several times acknowledged to be available by the Constitution, was, in fact, unconstitutional. Reasoning of this sort assumes that those who adopted the *Bill of Rights* had an intuition of a more encompassing right they were unable to articulate, but had to settle for a list of specific guarantees. In this view, the Court must finish the drafting by discerning a meaning that the framers could not. The word "hubris" comes to mind.

The Court has used its invented privacy right exclusively to enforce sexual freedoms. The most drastic instance was the success of the pro-abortion movement in evading democratic processes to lodge its desires in the Constitution, effectively making abortion a convenient birth control technique. The majority opinion in *Roe* v. *Wade* (1973) is a curious performance: in just over fifty-one pages it contains no shred of legal reasoning (or logic of any description), but simply announces that the right of privacy is sufficiently capacious to encompass a woman's right to an abortion. The opinion laid down new rules more permissive than any state legislature had produced. For once, the public did not passively acquiesce. The decision polarized American politics, including the politics of confirming nominees to the Supreme Court. Almost twenty years later the bitter dispute *Roe* began has not subsided, despite an explicit warning by three Justices in *Planned Parenthood* v. *Casey* (1992) that, if the public did not accept the Court's ruling, it would be derelict in its civic duty: "[T]he Court's interpretation of the Constitution calls the contending sides of a national controversy to end their national division by accepting a common mandate rooted in the Constitution.... [T]o overrule under fire in the absence of the most compelling reason ... would subvert the Court's legitimacy.... Some cost will be paid by anyone who approves or implements a constitutional decision where it is [unpopular]. An extra price will be paid by those who themselves disapprove of the decision's results when viewed outside of constitutional terms, but who nevertheless struggle to accept it, because they respect the rule of law. To all those who will be so tested by following, the Court implicitly undertakes to remain steadfast." It is mind-boggling that the citizenry were admonished that they should accept *Roe* because they must "respect the rule of law" when *Roe* itself, as well as *Casey*, are themselves crass violations of the rule of law, are not rooted in any conceivable interpretation of the Constitution, and have nothing to do with "constitutional terms." Yet it is the people who must pass the test set by the Court, reminding us of Bertolt Brecht's jest that the people have lost the confidence of the government and a new people must be formed.

Something of the intellectual rigor of the joint opinion may be gleaned from its now-famous "mystery passage": "[Our] law affords constitutional protection to... the most intimate and personal choices a person may make in a lifetime, choices central to personal dignity and autonomy, [which] are central to the liberty protected by the Fourteenth Amendment. At the heart of liberty is the right to define one's own concept of existence, of meaning, of the universe, and of the mystery of human life." The words are devoid of any ascertainable meaning. They could as easily be used to protect the unborn child's right to define his or her concept of existence. Some lower court judges have, nevertheless, found that the rhetoric compels such things as a right to assisted suicide, though their decisions were quickly reversed. What justifies either the creation of that right to assisted suicide or its denial is not clear from the mystery passage.

Worse was to come. In *Stenberg* v. *Carhart* (2000) the Court majority struck down a Nebraska statute prohibiting partial birth abortions. The procedure Nebraska sought to outlaw involves delivering the body of a baby, but leaving its head inside the uterus. The abortionist forces a pair of blunt scissors into the base of the skull, spreads the scissors to enlarge the opening, removes the scissors, and thrusts a suction catheter into the hole and evacuates the skull's contents. The skull collapses and the dead baby is fully removed from the mother. The Court majority held the procedure constitutionally protected, saying the statute was so imprecise that other forms of abortion might be "unduly burdened." That objection, were it accurate, would leave room for statutes more carefully drafted, but the Nebraska law was also found defective because, though it contained an exception for cases where the mother's life would otherwise be endangered, there was no exception for adverse effects on the mother's health. Even physicians who used the procedure said it was never necessary to preserve health, but the Court insisted on an exception that entirely swallows the rule: an abortionist will always say that this procedure is necessary to the woman's mental or emotional well-being.

Stenberg was by no means the end of the Court's campaign. *Hill* v. *Colorado* (2000) upheld a Colorado statute making it criminal to approach within 8 feet of a person seeking an abortion or within 100 feet of the entrance to an abortion clinic in order to protest or persuade against abortion. Because the ban was based on the content of the message, the Court's previous decisions showed it to be invalid. The statute would not have been countenanced for a moment had the speech been made against a war or in support of a strike. As a dissent noted, "There is apparently no end to the distortion of our First Amendment law that the Court is willing to endure to sustain this restriction upon the free speech of abortion opponents." Yet Justice Stevens stated with satisfaction in *Stenberg* that "the central holding of *Roe* v. *Wade*...has been endorsed by all but 4 of the 17 Justices who have

addressed the issue." Since there is no constitutional support for *Roe*, that fact is less a testimony to the merits of
the decision than proof that a large majority of the
Justices are willing to jettison the Constitution when
their own sympathies or ideologies are in play. Abortion
has become a sacred cause for the Court, before which
neither the Constitution nor the Court's previous decisions can stand. The abortion right has survived many
changes in the Court's personnel and, though it will
never gain general public assent, abortion virtually on
demand and for any reason seems secure for the foreseeable future. It is a central part of the New Class's creed.

Substantive Equal Protection and Homosexuality
Substantive due process is only one technique of activism
in the Court's repertoire. More recently, the Fourteenth
Amendment's guarantee of equal protection of the law,
designed to protect the newly freed slaves after the Civil
War, has become another uncontrollable source of judicial power. Since all law makes distinctions, it is possible
to say that all law denies equal protection to persons on
the unfortunate side of the line that has been drawn. To
invalidate all such laws would make anarchy a constitutional requirement. The Court, therefore, has chosen
which interests are subject to equal protection analysis
and which not. Once again, the Court, rather than the
legislature, makes the law.

In the name of equal protection, the Court may be on
the verge of another extra-constitutional venture – the

normalization of homosexuality. Nothing in the Constitution speaks to the question. Historically, homosexual
conduct has been left to the moral decisions of the
people and their elected representatives. In *Bowers* v.
Hardwick (1986) the Court narrowly held, in keeping
with the long-standing constitutional understanding, that
a state may make homosexual sodomy a criminal offense.
The vote was only five to four, however, and one member of the majority later publicly regretted his vote.

The dissent by Justice Blackmun, which had come
within a hair of being the majority opinion, stated with
startling boldness and clarity that the informing principle
of the Constitution is radical individual autonomy.
Chastising the majority for arguing that prior privacy
right cases related to the protection of the family, Justice
Blackmun stated: "We protect those rights [associated
with the family] not because they contribute in some
direct and material way, to the general public welfare, but
because they form so central a part of an individual's life.
'[T]he concept of privacy embodies the "moral fact that a
person belongs to himself and not others nor to society as
a whole."'" No greater endorsement of radical individual
autonomy or of sentiment more disintegrative of society
has ever before been articulated in a constitutional opinion. The family has no value beyond its importance to the
individuals in it, which means, if it means anything, that
neither the husband nor the wife need stay in the relationship if greater personal gratification is to be found
elsewhere, whether through abandonment, adultery, or, if
one is finicky, divorce. If the individual belongs only to

himself, moreover, there is no moral obligation to obey the law or to take part in national defense; there is no obligation to family, neighbors, nation, society, or to anything outside one's own skin.

Ten years later the *Bowers* majority opinion was abandoned in *Romer* v. *Evans* (1996). A few cities in Colorado, reflecting the new political and cultural power of homosexuals, enacted ordinances prohibiting discrimination on grounds of sexual orientation as well as on grounds of race and sex. Even private persons who believe strongly that homosexual conduct is immoral or prohibited by religion were forbidden to act on those beliefs. In a statewide referendum, Coloradans adopted a constitutional provision that precluded local governments from making homosexuals a favored class. The Supreme Court, however, held that this denial of special status to homosexuals violated the Equal Protection Clause of the Fourteenth Amendment. The theory was that homosexuals were impermissibly burdened if they had to secure special protection, equivalent to that afforded racial minorities, at the state rather than the local level. The law could be explained, the Court said, only by animosity toward homosexuals. The opinion closed with the preposterous assertion that the amendment "classifies homosexuals not to further a proper legislative end but to make them unequal to everyone else."

To the contrary, every constitutional or statutory provision at the state or the federal level does what the Colorado amendment did – it removes from some groups the capacity to alter the law at the local level. If one took the Court's majority's assertions seriously, as a dissent noted, state constitutional provisions prohibiting polygamy would violate the equal protection principle. Since certain states were admitted to the Union only on condition that they have such prohibitions that could not be revoked without the consent of the United States, would-be polygamists would have to persuade the entire nation, and not simply the voters of a single state. Matters are even worse than that, however. Under what appears to be the majority's rationale, it is difficult to see how any state or federal statute could be constitutional. They all remove discretion from localities. Since the Court has now held that the denial of special status to homosexuals is unconstitutional, *Bowers* probably must be taken to have been silently overruled.

The Court paused in its normalization of homosexuality in *Boy Scouts of America* v. *Dale* (2000). By the narrowest of margins the Court held that the Boy Scouts, which it called an "expressive association," have the right under the Speech Clause of the First Amendment to bar an open and activist homosexual from serving as an assistant scout master. Homosexuality was viewed as inconsistent with the morality the Scouts sought to inculcate. The Court overturned the judgment of the New Jersey Supreme Court which required, by strained reasoning, the retention of an assistant scoutmaster under a state law banning discrimination on the basis of sexual orientation in places of public accommodation. The author of the dissenting opinion, Justice Stevens, offered one argument disavowed by the other three dissenters. He called the popular disapproval of homosexuals "atavistic"and "nourished by sectarian doctrine"; the Boy Scouts' policy was "the product of habitual ways of thinking about strangers"; and, he concluded: "If we would guide by the light of reason, we must let our minds be bold." The other dissenters rightly observed: "Whether the group [whose policy is challenged] appears to be in the vanguard or rearguard of social thinking is irrelevant to the group's rights." Correct as that proposition undoubtedly is, it is difficult to reconcile with the Court's general practice where "vanguard" – New Class – social thinking is involved. It is tempting to think that the Court majority believed that opening the Boy Scouts to an adult homosexual activist would frame a general rule courting seduction and pederasty in other cases, a possibility the public would not accept.

Some state courts besides New Jersey's are ahead of federal courts in enacting the program of the intelligentsia under state constitutions. The high courts of Hawaii and Vermont, for example, have held same-sex marriages or the equivalent to be a right guaranteed by their state constitutions. The Vermont Constitution was adopted in 1793, and it is impossible to imagine that its ratifiers intended to invalidate any law that recognized marriage as a contract between a man and a woman only. The Hawaiian public responded with an amendment to their constitution overturning the decision; Vermont's constitution is quite difficult to amend and the legislature capitulated and enacted something called a "civil union," which carries the same benefits as marriage. Sooner or later the U.S. Supreme Court will be presented with the issue, and the outcome is far from clear.

Radical Feminism

Radical feminism, an increasingly powerful force across the full range of American institutions, overrode the Constitution in *United States* v. *Virginia* (1996). The Court held, seven votes to one, that the Equal Protection Clause required the Virginia Military Institute to admit women. VMI had been an all-male military college for over 150 years and had coexisted peaceably with the Equal Protection Clause for 128 of those years. VMI provided "adversative methods" of training, a program that was extremely rigorous mentally, physically, and emotionally. The admission of women is changing the nature of the institution. Minor changes in atmosphere are due to such things as the need for separate bathrooms, curtains on barrack windows, and the relaxation of discipline (so that young men who need rigorous discipline can no longer receive it at VMI). More serious is the new applicability of Title IX, the federal law dealing with sex discrimination. Sexual harassment, whether real or marginal, is now a major issue, as it is at almost all coeducational schools. Surveillance has been increased, though perhaps not sufficiently: VMI is experiencing the novelty of a pregnant cadet and is now under fire for proposing to dismiss both the woman and the man who caused the pregnancy. Not surprisingly, cadets no longer interact as before. Camaraderie has declined as young men, fearful of harassment charges, often avoid speaking to women. Women who can do six pullups are accepted as equals by male cadets, but the large majority of women who cannot are rebuffed. Whether one views these changes as wholesome or otherwise, it is clear that the VMI decision substantially changed the nature of the institution. After the service academies at West Point and Annapolis admitted women, they too had to relax their training standards to accommodate the mixed student body.

In his dissent in *United States* v. *Virginia*, Justice Scalia destroyed the majority's argument:

> Much of the Court's opinion is devoted to deprecating the close-mindedness of our forbears with regard to women's education, and even with regard to the treatment of women in areas that have nothing to do with education.... The virtue of a democratic system with a First Amendment is that it readily enables the people, over time, to be persuaded that what they took for granted is not so, and to change their laws accordingly. That system is destroyed if the smug assurances of each age are removed from the democratic process and written into the Constitution. So to counterbalance the Court's criticism of our ancestors, let me say a word in their praise: they left us free to change. The same cannot be said of this most illiberal Court, which has embarked on a course of inscribing one after another of the current preferences of the society (and in some cases only the

counter-majoritarian preferences of the society's
law-trained elite) into our Basic Law.

Scalia understated the anti-democratic course the Court
has taken. The Justices are not inscribing smug assur-
ances or the current preferences of our society into the
Constitution; those preferences are embodied in the
laws the Court declares unconstitutional. The counter-
majoritarian preferences adopted by the Court, moreover, are not simply those of a law-trained elite, but those
of a wider cultural elite. If only a law-trained elite were
involved, the Court would lack the support necessary to
enable it to revolutionize the culture.

VMI is only one example of a feminized Court transforming the Constitution. Feminists and their allies persuaded Congress to propose for state ratification an Equal
Rights Amendment requiring governments to treat men
and women equally: "Equality of rights under the law
shall not be denied or abridged by the United States or
by any State on account of sex." There was an initial wave
of state ratifications. Who could argue that women
should be treated less favorably than men? But sober second thought caused people to realize that men and
women cannot be treated identically in all respects. And
few wanted judges to make the delicate and evolving cultural distinctions and to freeze their musings into constitutional law. The no-difference principle made eminent
sense applied to different races. Black, Asian, and white
persons can be treated identically by government, but
men and women cannot – or at least nobody wants that

outcome. There appears to be a remarkable lack of enthusiasm for such innovations as integrated bathrooms or women on submarines.

The ERA was not ratified by the requisite number of states, even though feminists persuaded Congress to enlarge the time for ratification to make success more likely. The subject might have been thought closed, but it was not. The Supreme Court, using the Equal Protection Clause, has, case by case, effectively enacted the substance of the ERA. The Court is, in fact, cementing into place through constitutional rulings the current views of the Justices and the New Class as to the proper relationship of men and women in our culture. The *VMI* decision is only the most egregious of many such cases enacting the rejected ERA and thereby deforming the Constitution.

Lifestyle Socialism

The evolution of the American Supreme Court over the past three-quarters of a century has matched the change in New Class interests. If we follow Kenneth Minogue in identifying the culture war as dividing those favoring and those opposing the socialist ideal or impulse, then, as he points out, the movement has been away from socialism as a guide in economic affairs to a socialism of the culture – "lifestyle" socialism. That is one useful way of marking the distinction between the Court majority under Chief Justice Earl Warren and the current Court majority.

The Warren Court was the most political and imperialistic in American history, politicizing every area of law it touched, from antitrust and tax rulings to patent and administrative rulings and on to criminal procedures – and then, of course, to the Constitution. Constitutional or statutory text, legislative intent, precedent, considerations of the separation of powers and the justiciability of issues meant, if not nothing, then next to it. Regardless of precedent or doctrine, the observer knew that the antitrust defendant, the taxpayer, and the patentee would lose, as would a great deal of criminal law enforcement. Politics was a sure guide to outcomes; law was not.

The current Supreme Court is different. It is no longer devoted to economic equality. On subjects like antitrust and taxes, the meat and potatoes topics of the law, this Court is lawyerlike, highly skilled, and politically neutral. The Court no longer displays socialist tendencies in such areas. When a cultural or lifestyle issue is raised in a constitutional context, however, the approach changes: one bloc of four moves invariably to the cultural left and usually picks up at least a fifth vote, to drive the law in that direction. The victories for the jurisprudential conservatives tend to be narrow and defensive. They sometimes manage to keep the law from moving further left – for the time being – but do not restore the law as it was before liberal activism wrought its changes. What we call conservatism on the Court is usually a mere holding action; the liberals set the agenda and the conservatives resist, but rarely roll back prior liberal rulings or advance any agenda of their own. The result is a steady movement, occasionally delayed for the moment, of the Constitution to the cultural left.

The Illegitimacy of Judicial Activism

Judicial activism – the ordering of results not supported by any reasonable interpretation of the Constitution – may be rampant, but it is completely insupportable. Numerous attempts at justification have been made by academic lawyers and by left-wing activist groups such as the American Civil Liberties Union and, more recently, by heated statements from leaders of the American Bar Association. That swing should not be surprising. Some people will always rally around a center of power, particularly if it is the center most accessible to them and it produces the results they want. They are what the Canadian analysts F.L. Morton and Rainer Knopff refer to in their country as the "Court Party."

The defenses of activism are, despite their pedigree, remarkably simplistic. Departures from the actual Constitution are justified on several grounds: we are so far removed from the framers that the words they used either cannot be understood or have little relevance to us today; there is no reason why the present generation should be governed by men long dead; and we have a "living Constitution" that must be kept abreast of our evolving morality. None of these justifications has any merit whatever.

If it were true that we cannot understand the meaning of the Constitution, the only conclusion that follows is that judges should not exercise any power of judicial review. There would then be no basis for any statement that a statute did not comport with the Constitution, which, according to this argument, is incomprehensible.

The judge who nevertheless finds a statute invalid has no basis for that conclusion – unless his unsupported preferences are sufficient. Nobody takes the argument that far. In any event, it is not true that the Constitution has no meaning available to us. Aside from the words of the text, there are the records of the Philadelphia Convention, the state ratifying conventions, and the voluminous written exchanges between the Federalists who favored adoption and the anti-Federalists who opposed it.

As to the second contention, we are not governed by men long dead unless we desire to shrink or abandon the liberties they specified in the *Bill of Rights*. If we want additional liberties, that may be accomplished by constitutional amendment or by statute. Nothing in the Constitution prevents today's citizens from enacting statutes that specify additional liberties. Most of our guaranteed freedoms are statutory rather than constitutional. One need think only of the statutes governing civil rights, nondiscrimination, labor relations, the rights of the disabled, and so on, to see that point.

The "living Constitution" argument usually proceeds from the observation that society's morality is evolving and that the Constitution should be interpreted by the courts to reflect that fact. The argument is disingenuous. When a court invalidates a statute, it invalidates the best evidence available of what the society's morality entails. The evolving morality rationale, which the Supreme Court has used a number of times, is actually no more than a statement that the Court believes the morality it prefers should be enforced. The society is not evolving, only the Court is.

Nobody advances such spurious arguments to justify the Supreme Court in changing the meaning of a statute. These arguments are advanced only with respect to the Constitution, because a constitutional ruling cannot be overturned by the legislature. That fact reveals the anti-democratic animus, the socialist impulse, that lies behind each of these arguments for a Court that is not bound by the original understanding of the Constitution's principles.

Possible Remedies for Judicial Activism

It is not apparent what, if anything, can be done to bring the American judiciary back to legitimacy in a polity whose basic character and assumptions are democratic. There appear to be four possible routes, none of them encouraging at present, though they differ in the degree to which they offer long-run hope.

There are, first, two structural solutions that have drawn support from time to time. One is the proposal to resort to Article III, section 2, which provides that "the Supreme Court shall have appellate Jurisdiction...with such Exceptions, and under such Regulations as the Congress shall make." (There is no doubt that Congress may limit the jurisdiction of the lower federal courts.) The power to make exceptions to the Court's jurisdiction, however, is not a means to reassert democratic control, and it can hardly have been designed for that purpose. If the Supreme Court's jurisdiction were removed from a category of cases, jurisdiction would remain in the various state courts under Article VI's provision that the judges in every state shall be bound by the Constitution. Neither Congress nor the state legislatures, therefore, have the authority to remove constitutional cases from state courts. Removing all federal jurisdiction over, say, abortion cases would accomplish little or nothing. To do so would create the possibility of fifty different constitutional laws on the topic, and experience shows that many state courts are even more activist than their federal counterparts.

A second structural solution would require a constitutional amendment to permit the overruling of Supreme Court decisions by the full Congress or by the Senate. Suggestions of this sort have been made from time to time, but are never taken very seriously. Canada's *Charter of Rights and Freedoms* has a similar provision, as will be seen, but so far it has not proved effective in curbing its Supreme Court. Perversely, it may even encourage activism by allowing Canadian judges to claim increased freedom to innovate precisely on the grounds that they are subject to democratic revision if they are seen to go too far. Canadian legislatures only rarely use their power to override.

There remain two other possible cures for judicial encroachment on democratic prerogatives. One lies in the appointment of judges who will apply the Constitution according to the original understanding of its principles. So far this strategy has not been successful. Once on the Court, appointees often display unsuspected liberal activist tendencies or they gradually move in that direction because of the influence of the media and the academic world on judicial reputations. Moreover, federal court, and particularly Supreme Court, confirmations have become a major battleground in the culture war. The Democratic Party is now the ally of the New Class, so that, in a closely divided or a Democratic Senate, nominees suspected of adhering to the judicial philosophy of original understanding are unlikely to win confirmation. Nevertheless, the attempt to change views about proper judging and to confirm candidates with those views, unsuccessful though it has been and bleak as are its prospects in the immediate future, may be the only chance to divert the Court from antidemocratic activism in the service of liberal cultural aggression.

The second nonstructural cure for judicial usurpation of the democratic process is to persuade the Court itself to mend its ways, but so far any such effort has proved utterly ineffective. The Justices appear to be impervious to argument. They make no attempt whatever to answer the criticisms leveled against their conduct. There was a time when academic lawyers worried about the counter-majoritarian nature of judicial review and the absence of any checks upon the Court. The only protection they found lay in the notion that the Supreme Court Justices are confined by tradition. That is all there was or ever could be, according to Alexander Bickel, though, by the time of the Warren Court, even that tradition, he said, had been shattered. I am not sure there ever was much of a tradition capable of confining the Court. There may have been a degree of restraint arising from apprehension about the reaction of the public, the profession, and the other institutions of government. But now, whatever tradition there was, has indeed been broken and any lingering apprehension has been dissipated by the inertia of political opposition.

In any event, it was said that the Court would be kept to a proper path by the necessity that it justify its decisions by tight reasoning that connected those results to the text and history of the Constitution. If its reasoning faltered, if it displayed will rather than judgment, it would be brought back to its duty by the informal criticism of the bar. That assurance turned out to be an idle fancy. The bar now resembles a collection of businessmen interested only in maximizing profit, rather than a body of professionals interested in maintaining the integrity of the judicial role. Indeed, the bar tends to identify with the courts and to resent any criticism of them. Daniel Troy has collected examples. So far sunk in Court worship is the American Bar Association – once a professional group, now a liberal political faction – that its president could say: "An attack on activist judges is an attack on our Constitution. It is an attack on our tripartite system of government." Another claimed that critics of the judiciary are "taking a page out of George Wallace's playbook" – meaning that the critics are irresponsible demagogues. He compared politicians who criticize activist courts to Communist Party officials in the Ukraine who demanded that judges phone them to be told what results to reach. We are, the ABA informs us, in crises that threaten judicial independence. One ABA official proposed professional discipline, including disbarment, for politicians who are also lawyers and who criticize judges.

The legal academies are even worse, not only defending judicial imperialism but devising theories justifying further incursions on territory rightfully belonging to democratic government.

The bar, one must conclude, is today incapable of the disinterested evaluation of judicial performance that we once thought would be a check on runaway courts. There seems to be no institutional check on activist judges. Nor is there any prospect of such a check so long as courts, the organized bar, the legal academy, and the media form a Court Party serving the interests of the New Class to which they belong.

This necessarily scanty review of the American Court's activist rewritings of the Constitution has touched only a tiny number of such decisions. One would suppose that the Court or some of its members would by now have undertaken a justification for such radical and habitual activism. The obtrusive and uncomfortable fact is that the Court has never offered a justification of its practice of using the Constitution to alter and reverse the understanding of the framers and ratifiers of the Constitution. Though it is certainly peculiar, if not perverse, to use a document that is the sole source of the Court's authority to subvert the document itself, most of the Justices quite obviously feel no need to explain the legitimacy of that course. The most the Court has ever offered is the observation that the Court has never felt its power confined to the intended meaning of the Constitution. That much is apparent, but a long habit of abusing power can never make the abuse legitimate. That is particularly so when the representative branches of government have no effective way of resisting the Court. The Justices seem to think that their persistent invasions of turf belonging to democratic rule have established an easement across the Constitution for their personal predilections.

All these trends might have been predicted, and some opponents of ratification did, in fact, predict them. Given unchecked power, most human beings, even those in robes, will abuse it. In the absence of any democratic counterweight, we must rely on the self-restraint of the Justices. These days, that virtue rarely musters five votes.

2

CANADA

Rights-based judicial review taken to its extreme becomes an anti-democratic power, wielded by courts to alter the fundamental character of a nation's constitution without significant popular participation or even public awareness. . . . Judicial supremacy, in other words, is overtaking constitutional supremacy.

Christopher P. Manfredi

Changes in the legal realm, however, have been accompanied by a general failure of the political process to recognize the rights of lesbians and gays without the pressure of court decisions behind them.

Justice Claire L'Heureux-Dubé

Judicial review based on constitutionally protected rights and liberties did not become a feature of government in Canada until the adoption of the *Charter of Rights and Freedoms* in 1982. For that reason, this type of judicial review did not follow the same trajectory in Canada as in the United States. There has been no period in which the post-*Charter* Canadian Supreme Court has responded primarily to the ideology of the business class. By 1982 the New Class's outlook had become dominant and the Court's activism, which began with the *Charter*, at once responded to the values of that class. The Court has continued on that path ever since.

Canadian constitutional law does not simply replicate the American version, but it displays the same overall tendencies. This resemblance is not primarily because of American influence, but because the same liberal intelligentsia dominates the jurisprudence of both countries. The Canadian Supreme Court is producing a constitutional jurisprudence that is interesting in both its parallels to and its differences from that produced by the United States Supreme Court. Although the Canadian Court seems the more sensible of the two in cases touching on freedom of speech and freedom of religion, in other cases, notably those relating to abortion and homosexuality, that Court is strikingly activist, perhaps more so than its American counterpart.

Before the adoption of the Canadian *Charter*, Canadian courts interpreted the statutory *Bill of Rights* in light of its text and its history. As a result, judges were relatively restrained and the traditional understandings of rights were preserved. The adoption of the *Charter*, however, emboldened judges and introduced the era of judicial activism. For the first time the judiciary vigorously used its authority to strike down laws that infringed on what the judges themselves considered fundamental rights not mentioned in the *Charter*. It was then that the powers of self-government gradually began to give way to the reality of judicial governance. As F.L. Morton and Rainer Knopff put it, "The fact that the Charter revolution is more a judicial than a legal revolution is evident in the many cases that brought about dramatic legal change without any textual warrant for such change."

The substance of the *Charter*, though differently expressed, is similar to that of the American *Bill of Rights*. Section 2 of the *Charter* lists four fundamental freedoms: freedom of conscience and religion; freedom of thought, belief, opinion, and expression, including freedom of the press and other media of communication; freedom of peaceful assembly; and freedom of association. Sections 7 through 14 list Legal Rights, such as "the right to life, liberty and security of the person and the right not to be deprived thereof except in accordance with the principles of fundamental justice." Also named are such rights as security against unreasonable search or seizure and procedural rights of various kinds relating to arrest, trial, and cruel and unusual punishment.

Section 15 deals with Equality Rights. It first grants a right to equal protection and equal benefit of the law without discrimination based on race, national or ethnic origin, color, religion, sex, age, or mental or physical disability.

Those rights are at once heavily qualified by the following subsection, which says that freedom from discrimination "does not preclude any law, program or activity that has as its object the amelioration of conditions of disadvantaged individuals or groups including those that are disadvantaged because of race, national or ethnic origin, colour, religion, sex, age or mental or physical disability." That subsection takes back much or even most of the equality the first part of section 15 promises. "Amelioration" means preferential treatment for the groups named, and preferential treatment means discrimination against the groups not named. The major group not named is, of course, healthy, heterosexual, white, Canadian-born males. It is disquieting, to say the least, to find permission for governmental discrimination written into the nation's basic law.

The *Charter*'s rights and freedoms are not absolute and section 1 attempts to specify their limits:

> The *Canadian Charter of Rights and Freedoms* guarantees the rights and freedoms set out in it subject only to such reasonable limits prescribed by law as can be demonstrably justified in a free and democratic society.

In applying the *Charter*, courts first determine whether a law entails a *prima facie* violation of the basic rights specified by the *Charter*. If a violation is found, the court must then decide whether the infringement can be upheld as a "reasonable limit" that is "demonstrably justified" in a "free and democratic society." On its face, this provision does not distinguish judging under the *Charter* from judging under the U.S. Constitution. An American judge applying the Speech Clause of the First Amendment, for example, understands that the statement that Congress (or any other branch of the federal or state government) "shall make no law...abridging the freedom of speech" cannot literally mean that government may not interfere with speech in any way. American courts balance the value of freedom of speech against other social goods and have held, for example, that the amendment does not destroy the law of libel and that time, place, and manner restrictions are appropriate – loudspeakers blasting political messages at midnight in a residential neighborhood may be banned.

The explicit language of section 1 of the *Charter* actually gives precious little guidance when it states that an infringement of a freedom is valid if it is reasonable and demonstrably justified in a free and democratic society. The *Charter* assumes that courts will review the legislature's work *de novo*, without, that is, any weight given to the fact that the law to be judged as democratic or not was, in fact, enacted democratically. Section 1 of the *Charter* does not require or encourage the Canadian courts to give any presumption of legality to a law that arguably encroaches on a specified freedom. While American courts do speak of such a presumption, the presumption often appears to be a rote recitation rather than a factor with real weight in the judiciary's deliberations.

Canadian courts are more apt to receive and weigh social and economic evidence. The Canadian judicial practice is often almost indistinguishable from what

Canadian legislatures do. Canadian judges make many decisions by weighing technical or social factors that lie well outside their professional training. Thus, Canada's federal government enacted a law limiting the advertising of tobacco products. The Supreme Court found the law to be an unjustified limitation on freedom of expression as protected by the *Charter of Rights* and was, therefore, null and void. In that case, the Court had to draw conclusions about the link between advertising and tobacco use, the physical harm caused by smoking, and related matters that are frequently the subject of scientific dispute. These are all issues that the Court considers with the assistance, or perhaps the handicap, of highly technical information and testimony thrust upon it by the contending sides. This deliberation duplicates the vast efforts already undertaken by the various committees and subcommittees supporting the legislative and executive branches.

There are several procedures, some designed by the Supreme Court, that increase judicial power at the expense of self-government. Canada has, for example, a legislatively created reference procedure that allows Canadian governments to present legal issues directly to appeal courts for rulings on constitutionality. There need be no actual litigation to justify the reference,[1] so the judges must rule on abstract questions without the sharpened focus provided by seeing the operation of a law in a factual setting. The reference procedure is, however, often a convenient way for elected representatives to shed highly controversial and inconvenient political disagreements by calling them legal issues and shifting the decision to the courts. The politics of "issue avoidance" is highly convenient to politicians, but its price is the suppression of public debate and government accountability.

A sure sign that a judiciary has decided that its function is not simply to decide controversies between litigants, but to legislate for society generally, is the abandonment of constraints that distinguish a court from an elected body. It will be recalled that the U.S. Supreme Court dropped the requirement that parties have standing to litigate the issues they wish to present – that the law or the practice in question has a direct impact upon them – only with respect to the Establishment Clause, so that the Court could ensure that no trace of religion is left in the public sphere. When the discipline of the standing doctrine is removed, the Court effectively issues an invitation to ideologically motivated persons and groups to test every government policy. Litigants invariably respond. As the requirements of standing are weakened, judicial power grows in proportion to that loss. Canada provides many examples of this axiom.

Thorson v. *Canada* (1975), for example, held that

---

[1]   *The Justices of the U.S. Supreme Court rejected such a procedure over two hundred years ago. In July 1793 Secretary of State Thomas Jefferson wrote to the Justices at the direction of President George Washington seeking their opinion on the propriety of their giving advice on a number of legal questions arising, or likely to arise, as a consequence of the war in Europe. A few weeks later the Justices declined to give the opinions sought, essentially on separation-of-powers grounds. The impropriety of advisory opinions remains to this day a basic limitation on the authority of the federal courts.*

taxpayers could seek a declaration of the constitutional invalidity of a statute without having to show that its enforcement would inflict harm on them. In *Minister of Justice (Canada)* v. *Borowski* (1981), a case concerning abortion, the Court said that standing to challenge legislation could be given to individuals who showed they had "a general interest in the validity of the legislation and that there is no other reasonable and effective manner in which the issue may be brought before the Court." These invitations to the public at large ensure that no domestic issue will avoid judicial rather than political resolution.

So, too, with respect to the concept of mootness. If a controversy becomes academic, in the pejorative sense of that term – because the parties settled their differences, the situation changed so that the complaining party had nothing left to complain about, or the plaintiff died, effectively removing his interest in the outcome of a dispute – a court, acting as an adjudicator of real disputes, would ordinarily declare the matter moot and dismiss the case. Not so the Canadian Court, which rules in cases where the plaintiff no longer has a personal stake. It is difficult to explain this process on any hypothesis other than that the Court is more interested in governing the society than in doing justice to identifiable litigants. It must be conceded that the U.S. Supreme Court has, on occasion, behaved like the Canadian Court. This was true most notably of the Court headed by Chief Justice Earl Warren, but since that time the doctrines of standing and mootness have undergone at least a modest revival.

These doctrines serve several salutary functions. A live

controversy by a person with a personal stake in the outcome, for example, makes more likely the full exploration
of the issue and an awareness of particular circumstances
that illuminate the hazards as well as the benefits of a
general rule. But the main value of these doctrines is that
they tend to confine a court to the resolution of specific
controversies rather than allowing the judges to enter a
competition with the legislature in which the courts
have the advantage of being almost always final. Courts
work at a disadvantage in that a real legislature receives
not only written and oral presentations, as does a court,
but also intensive lobbying by groups with a variety of
special interests at stake. This process informs the legislators of general considerations as well as specific circumstances that do not fit the law's generalizations and the
complications they may present. If a court wishes to displace the legislature as the ultimate rule maker, it ought
to open its members to lobbying by the parties or interested members of the public.

The dilemma posed when a court makes policy at
large, independent of the desires of the parties, was nicely
illustrated in a U.S. antitrust case. While litigation challenging a merger was pending before the Supreme Court,
the parties settled the dispute. The Court should have dismissed the case as moot, but, instead, expressing dissatisfac-
tion with the settlement, remanded the case for further
proceedings below. At that point a lawyer for the defendant approached Justice Brennan, an old friend, in his
chambers. The Justice, offended, told the man to leave, and
the lawyer was subject to general condemnation for his

action. The episode could be viewed in another light, however. The lawyer realized there was nobody on the other side of the dispute but the Court and he tried to settle the case with the only opponent his client had. If courts are to be legislatures, perhaps such *ex parte*, or interested, practice should be encouraged rather than reprehended.

To add further to its power as a political organ, the Canadian Court has ruled that not merely the holdings of a case but any general observations made in passing – what lawyers call *obiter dicta* – are law binding on lower courts, and hence on society. In this decision, too, it surpasses the activism of United States courts, which usually preserve the distinction between the reasoning that is essential to the decision and the language used more or less offhandedly in the same opinion. In the United States, *dicta* may be valuable guides to the court's likely rulings in later cases, but such language is not binding. It may be contradicted by a lower court when the case seems to demand it, and may be distinguished or disavowed by the Supreme Court itself.

In an era of increasing judicial imperialism, Canada's *Charter* is, in one respect, clearly superior to the U.S. Constitution. The *Charter* provides some democratic control over courts in section 33: "Parliament or the legislature of a province may expressly declare in an Act of Parliament or of the legislature, as the case may be, that the Act or provision thereof shall operate notwithstanding a provision included in section 2 or sections 7 to 15 of this Charter." A "notwithstanding" declaration has a life of five years and may be renewed.

Section 33 has largely fallen into disuse. Though the section has been used by two other provinces, its fall into disfavor was due in large part to a controversial use of the clause by Quebec. Yet, as Professor Christopher Manfredi points out, the clause is "a legitimate instrument for preventing the slide from constitutional to judicial supremacy." Judging from experience with judicial review in Westernized nations, that slide seems inevitable where there is no effective democratic check on the judiciary. There is no particular reason, and no warrant in democratic or constitutional theory, for a supreme court to supersede the principles of the constitution that alone gives the court authority to void legislative acts: that is, to seize power and reject responsibility. Manfredi argues that section 33 could be improved by requiring that it be used only after a court decision, and not beforehand, as a means of insulation from any review. Furthermore, he urges that the vote required to invoke section 33 might be increased from the present simple majority in the House of Commons and the Senate to a three-fifths majority in each chamber.

It might be suggested, however, that the present relative ineffectiveness of the notwithstanding clause is not because it is too easy to use but because it has been made difficult to invoke owing to the cry that it interferes with judicial independence. That is an odd objection. The notwithstanding clause was built into the *Charter* at the outset precisely to establish a democratic limit to judicial independence. The cult of the robe, the near worship of courts, and the necessary reliance of the New Class on authoritarian rather than democratic rule seem the reasons for the decline of section 33 to a state approaching desuetude. If so, it would probably be a mistake to try to purchase respectability and renewed vitality for the clause by making it even more difficult to use.

Before I knew of Canada's attempt at a democratic curb, I once suggested something very like the notwithstanding clause of section 33 for the United States. That would, of course, require a constitutional amendment, and the chances of such a proposal being accepted lie somewhere between zero and nil. The suggestion was brushed aside as intolerably radical. In any event, I was persuaded that such an amendment would do little good because Canada's section 33, expressly designed to allow democratic intervention against runaway courts, has proved ineffective. The mystique of the courts is too great. In all probability, the mere existence of a checking power, even though ineffective in practice, would be used, as it has been in Canada, to justify judicial adventurism.

Though alike in many respects, Canada's Court has taken some markedly different courses than has the American Court. Interestingly enough, the Supreme Court of Canada, though by some measures more activist than the Supreme Court of the United States, has produced a less sweeping and a considerably more sensible law relating to freedom of speech and religion. A few cases make the point.

Freedom of Speech and Religion

The issue in *The Queen* v. *Keegstra* (1990) was the constitutionality of section 319(2) of the Criminal Code,
which prohibits the willful promotion of hatred against
identifiable groups. James Keegstra, an Alberta high
school teacher, was charged with expressing virulent
anti-Semitic statements to his students. He claimed the
right to do so under section 2(b) of the *Charter*, which
guarantees "freedom of thought, belief, opinion and
expression." The Court had no difficulty in finding an
infringement of section 2(b); Keegstra's statements were
clearly expression. The Court majority, however, felt
obliged to go into the matter further. Chief Justice
Dickson laid out the values of speech freedom: seeking
and attaining truth; participation in political and social
decision-making; and diversity in forms of individual
self-fulfillment and human flourishing. The third value
reflects a bias of the New Class and has, on more than one
occasion, led American courts astray. If self-fulfillment
and human flourishing in diverse forms is the object,
freedom of speech is entitled to no more solicitude than
freedom to engage in stock market speculation or to bet
on horse races. Humans have very different forms of self-
fulfillment and flourishing. Much expression that
American courts protect as contributing to self-fulfillment, or radical individualism, contributes to the coars-
ening of American culture and does not qualify as seeking
truth or participating in political and social decision-
making. The constitutional protection of an obscenity
in *Cohen* v. *California*, discussed in chapter 1, and other

rulings such as the protection of flag-burning can only be explained as manifesting a New Class delight in verbal and symbolic forms of self-gratification.

Having found that Keegstra's odious utterances were expression and thus, *prima facie*, protected, the Chief Justice turned to section 1 of the *Charter* to determine whether, in this case, application of the criminal law was demonstrably justified in a free and democratic society. He quoted an opinion by Justice Wilson that freedom of expression might have greater value in a political context than it does in the context of the disclosure of details in a marital dispute. This approach differs from the slavish devotion to freedom of speech and the press that led the American Court to rule, for example, that a newspaper had a right, superior to a state privacy law, to publish the name of a rape victim, a fact of no conceivable public interest.

The Chief Justice then turned to an examination of American constitutional law. He remarked that he would not have backed away as completely as the U.S. Court has done from the ruling in *Beauharnais* v. *Illinois* (1952). That case upheld against First Amendment challenge a state law forbidding certain types of group defamation. He found support for departing from the American view in the "special role given equality and multiculturalism in the Canadian Constitution" and in "the international commitment to eradicate hate propaganda."

Among the evils of hate speech that the opinion listed was their effect on society. Here the Chief Justice departed from the American Court's view. He quoted the Canadian Cohen Committee report (1965) to the effect that individuals can be persuaded to believe "almost any-thing" in certain circumstances and with the right techniques of communication. The committee said: "We are less confident in the 20th century that the critical faculties of individuals will be brought to bear on the speech and writing which is directed at them." The Chief Justice added that events "have qualified sharply our belief in the rationality of man."

That statement is a refreshing breath of realism to anyone familiar with free speech dogma in the United States. American law has been badly deformed by the irrebuttable presumption of unswerving rationality embodied in Justice Holmes's deadly metaphor of the "marketplace of ideas." The naive notion that, if all ideas are allowed in the marketplace, the best ones will ultimately and inevitably prevail is refuted by human history, including the history of democracies. Though human beings are frequently rational, they are, often enough, sufficiently irrational to contradict the Enlightenment notions of John Stuart Mill and Oliver Wendell Holmes. That is particularly true of the kind of emotional, assaultive speech that Keegstra employed. Then, as Alexander Bickel wrote, the marketplace is replaced by the bullring. Chief Justice Dickson pertinently quoted Justice Jackson's opinion in *Beauharnais*: "[S]inister abuses of our freedom of expression . . . can tear apart a society, brutalize its dominant elements, and persecute even to extermination, its minorities." The Chief Justice allowed that he was "very reluctant to attach anything but the highest importance to expression relevant to political matters. But given the unparalleled vigour with which hate propaganda repudiates and undermines democratic values, and in particular its condemnation of the view that all citizens need be treated with equal respect and dignity so as to make participation in the political process meaningful, I am unable to see the protection of such expression as integral to the democratic ideal so central to the s. 2(b) rationale."

Less encouraging was the Chief Justice's reliance on international human rights principles in assessing the legislative objective. It is uncertain to what degree legislators were motivated by consideration of the various documents enunciating those principles. A more fundamental objection is that, as we have reason to know, international declarations – in the United Nations, for example – are often so vague as to provide little guidance in actual cases, yet are quite as capable of being politically motivated and pernicious as they are of being humane and balanced. The opinion also cites a welter of academic writings in support of such legislation, thus explicitly endorsing New Class views. Judges ought to be wary of the literature produced by writers from the generally leftish academic world.

That element suggests a danger in the *Keegstra* ruling. Given the virulence of "political correctness" in the academic world, and in much of the New Class, it may be that the criminal law will come to be used to stifle even legitimate discussion of group and cultural differences. Those topics are necessarily central, for example, to any intelligent debate about immigration policy. Yet in many quarters such debate is now stamped as intolerably racist or hostile to particular ethnic groups. It remains to be seen whether prosecutors and courts will continue to resist this New Class trend and to maintain the distinction, sometimes subtle, between hate speech and legitimate discussion of group differences. If they cannot, it may turn out in the long run that the U.S. courts were inadvertently wise to back away from *Beauharnais* and to refuse to judge speech by its content.

The *Keegstra* opinion exemplifies an unfortunate characteristic exemplified in the constitutional opinions of almost all nations: complexity and length. There is no occasion here to discuss all the sub-issues the opinion addresses or the excruciating detail in which every issue and sub-issue is considered. Such opinions will not be read by the general public; they are useful almost solely to those whose professional preoccupation they are. The United States public has almost no idea what is in its Constitution, much less the doctrines of the Supreme Court, and there is little doubt that the Canadian public is similarly ill-informed. For the public at large, lengthy and tedious opinions tend to conceal, rather than to illuminate, constitutional reasoning.

Though the decision in *Keegstra* was split, the Court had no difficulty in *The Queen* v. *Sharpe* (2001) in finding unanimously that the prohibition of the "expression" embodied in child pornography was justified under section 1 of the *Charter.* Commercial speech was protected in *RJR–MacDonald Inc.* v. *Canada (Attorney-General)* (1995), holding, by a five-to-four vote, that the restrictions on tobacco advertising, promotion, and labeling contained in the *Tobacco Products Control Act* were not justified under section 1. This decision was greater protection of commercial speech than the U.S. Court has granted, though it is difficult to compare the decisions in the two countries because the American interpretation of the First Amendment in this context suffers from a long-standing judicial practice, only recently repudiated in part, of deferring to legislative regulation of commercial speech. To the degree that a central function of free speech is the search for truth, not just political truth but any social truth, the rationale and the history of the founders' respect for commercial speech argue for greater protection than has been accorded in the United States. Tobacco is undoubtedly a danger to health, but users know the possible consequences of their choice, and tobacco has other attributes – such as giving pleasure to individuals – and it hardly creates the same social dangers as hate speech or child pornography.

Religion

Religion is another area in which the Canadian Court differs from the U.S. Court. Canada shows none of the savage antagonism about religious questions that characterizes American constitutional law. *The Queen v. Big M Drug Mart Ltd.* (1985), a case over retail trading on Sunday, did not denounce any public recognition of religion, though it struck down the *Lord's Day Act*, a Sunday closing law, which made most forms of work and commercial activity on that day criminal. Justice Dickson, for the Court, reasoned that the Act violated section 2(a)'s guarantee of freedom of conscience and religion, which included nonbelief, because the Act coerced individuals to affirm a specific (Christian) belief. Resort to section 1 was unavailing. The first argument advanced, that the choice of day of rest adhered to by the Christian majority is the most practical, was "fundamentally repugnant because it would justify the law upon the very basis upon which it is attacked." The second argument, that the day of rest chosen might as well be the one traditionally observed, was rejected because it assigned a nonreligious motive to the legislature which was contrary to fact.

Jones v. *The Queen* (1986) upheld the conviction of the pastor of a fundamentalist church for violation of the Alberta *School Act* because he refused to send his children to public school and refused to seek the exemption provided if an appropriate government official certified that a pupil was receiving efficient instruction at home or elsewhere or if the pupil was attending a private school approved by the Department of Education. The Act was said to constitute some interference with freedom of religion, but did not infringe section 2(a) because alternatives were provided. Section 1 was of no avail to the pastor because the province's compelling interest in the adequate education of the young meant that the law was demonstrably justified in a free and democratic society. The result seems quite correct.

Though the claims of religion lost in *Big M Drug Mart* and *Jones*, those claims were treated respectfully and without the hyperventilation that the U.S. religion opinions often display. Often enough in Canada, moreover, the appeal to religious freedom prevails.

In *British Columbia College of Teachers* v. *Trinity Western University* (2001) the Court faced the necessity to resolve a conflict between two values, one explicitly found in the *Charter* and the other of its own creation. The conflict was between religious freedom and the preferred status the Court had created for homosexuals. Trinity Western University is a private institution associated with the Evangelical Free Church of Canada. It sought to have its students sign a "Community Standards" document agreeing to refrain from all biblically condemned practices, including drunkenness, profanity, abortion, premarital sex, adultery, and, the crux of the case, homosexual activity. The College of Teachers refused to accredit the university's education program on the grounds that it was discriminatory, rendering its students unfit to teach in the public school system. The university sued and the Supreme Court, dividing eight to one, ordered the College of Teachers to accredit the program.

The Court rejected the argument based on the equality rights of section 15: "To state that the voluntary adoption of a code of conduct based on a person's own religious beliefs, in a private institution, is sufficient to engage s. 15 would be inconsistent with freedom of conscience and religion, which co-exist with the right to equality." The College of Teachers could appropriately consider equality rights, but it was also required to consider, as it had not, the right of religious freedom. Neither right is absolute. "TWU's Community Standards, which are limited to prescribing conduct of members while at TWU, are not sufficient to support the conclusion that BCCT should anticipate intolerant behavior in the public schools. Indeed, if TWU's Community Standards could be sufficient in themselves to justify denying accreditation, it is difficult to see how the same logic would not result in the denial of accreditation to members of a particular church."

This is obviously not a case in which religious beliefs always trump the protection of homosexual conduct. Yet, given the American Supreme Court's hostility to religion and solicitude for homosexuality, it is easy to think the decision might well have gone the other way in the United States.

Abortion

Abortion occupies an identical position in the Canadian *Charter* and in the American Constitution: both documents are silent on the issue, leaving the dispute between the opposing forces for resolution in the political arena. Section 7 of the *Charter*, which protects the right to life and the right to liberty, can be appealed to by both the anti- and the pro-abortion factions. From the beginning, then, the Supreme Court should have stated that neither provision was enacted with abortion in mind, and that the *Charter*, having deliberately avoided the issue, had nothing to say and so the issue must remain with the legislature. In Canada, however, the anti-abortion side actively but futilely sought a Court ruling that the "right to life" guaranteed in section 7 of the *Charter* banned abortion. In the United States, pro-abortionists aggressively sought a ruling that abortion is a constitutional right and achieved victory in 1973 in *Roe* v. *Wade*. Anti-abortionists' argument that abortion is forbidden by the guarantee against the deprivation of life without due process of law in the Fifth and Fourteenth amendments has, predictably, met with no success.

The outcomes have been similar in Canada and the United States because feminists and their New Class allies in both countries overwhelmingly support abortion rights. Given the judicial identification in both countries with those groups, the pro-abortion side has won. The political response to the judicial encouragement of abortion has not been as different in Canada and the United States as might have been expected, given the *Charter's* notwithstanding clause – which, theoretically, is much more easily invoked than the American Constitution's difficult procedure for securing an amendment. Yet the capacity for effective political response in the two countries is about the same: nil. Once a supreme court has spoken, creating what it chooses to call a constitutional right, the psychological advantage swings, usually decisively, in favor of a position that had previously been unable to prevail in the legislature. Unless the government, national or provincial, is determined – unless restoring the previous position, the *status quo ante*, is an important part of its agenda (which in the case of abortion it never is) – the notwithstanding clause will remain unused and the pro-abortion forces will have won what they could not previously persuade the people and the legislature to accept. As a result, the number of abortions in Canada rose substantially, just as after *Roe* the rate increased spectacularly in the United States.

Knopff and Morton attribute the Canadian Court's altered willingness to accept the pro-abortion decision to more than the replacement of Canada's statutory *Bill of Rights* by the *Charter of Rights and Freedoms*. The latter, after all, was silent, and deliberately so, on the issue of abortion. The change by the Court, they point out, was due to the dramatic change in the social and political climate. Radical feminism had emerged as a major force in Canadian politics, and women secured seats on the Supreme Court as well as much greater participation in the legal profession. This is not to say that women are uniformly pro-abortion, but the women entering the legal profession, having attended university and law school, were members of the New Class, and they heavily favored abortion rights. In Canada as in America, immersion in higher education these days produces a pronounced swing to the cultural left.

In *Morgentaler, Smoling and Scott* v. *The Queen* (1988), four of the five Justices in the majority found procedural deficiencies in the statute regulating abortion, but Justice Wilson wrote that it would merely be a waste of Parliament's time to address procedures because women have a substantive right to abortion. She ignored the legislative history of section 7, perhaps because that history tended to contradict the position she espoused. In language remarkably similar to that of the American Justices

Blackmun (in *Roe*) and Brennan (in the contraceptive case, *Eisenstadt* v. *Baird* [1972]), and the joint opinion of O'Connor, Kennedy, and Souter (in *Planned Parenthood* v. *Casey*), she argued that section 7 promoted "human dignity and worth," guaranteeing "a degree of personal autonomy over important decisions intimately affecting their private lives." Like the American judges, Justice Wilson was unconcerned with what the persons who adopted the *Charter* understood themselves to be doing. Acknowledging that Parliament had an interest in protecting the fetus in the later stages of development, she offered her personal opinion that Parliament's power might become legitimate "somewhere in the second trimester."

Justice McIntyre dissented, saying "when in the name of constitutional interpretation, the Court adds something to the Constitution that was deliberately excluded from it, the Court in reality substitutes its view of what should be so for the amending process." That statement seems undeniable.

The anti-abortion forces proved equally ready to use the *Charter* for purposes it was not designed to encompass. In *Borowski* the plaintiff wanted the courts to declare that the same statute stricken in *Morgentaler* outlawed all abortions because of section 7's protection of "everyone" as entitled to life. But since the prior case had invalidated the statute, the Court, after hearing argument and a considerable subsequent delay, announced that the present nonexistence of the statute rendered Borowski's claim moot. Justice Sopinka's opinion for the Court said, with respect to standing, that it was sufficient that a plaintiff show that "he has a genuine interest as a citizen in the validity of the legislation" he challenges. In a word, ideology will suffice. Mootness, he said, requires that there be "no present live controversy" which "affects the rights of the parties." But "[t]he general policy or practice is enforced in moot cases unless the court exercises its discretion to depart from its policy or practice." "Discretion" seems to be a synonym for lawlessness.

That this is not too harsh a judgment is demonstrated by the Court's contrasting decision in *Daigle* v. *Tremblay* (1989). In this case Daigle, having broken with her lover, Tremblay, after five months of cohabitation, decided she wanted an abortion. She cited no reasons other than a desire not to have a child. Abortion here was clearly a form of second-thought birth control. (She had stopped taking contraceptive pills before conception and, for four months afterward, had made no effort to end her pregnancy.) Tremblay sued and was granted an injunction against the abortion under the Quebec *Charter of Human Rights*, whose right to life ran to "human beings" rather than the "persons" protected by the national *Charter* and was arguably broader – broad enough, in fact, to outlaw the killing of a fetus, which is a human being, whatever the legal status of a "person" might be. Daigle was eighteen weeks pregnant when she and Tremblay separated and the case began. The Quebec court's injunction was rushed to a hearing in the Supreme Court of Canada within one month.

On the day in question, when the Justices reconvened after a morning of argument, they were told by Daigle's counsel that he had just learned that his client had gone ahead with the abortion in the United States. She had then been pregnant for just over five months. The reasoning of *Borowski* would indicate that the case was moot, but the Court decided to defer decision of that issue and went on with the hearing. Less than two hours after the conclusion of arguments, the Court announced that it was vacating the injunction and would issue an opinion later. After three months it did. The fetus was found not to have a right to life under the Quebec *Charter* because the framers had elected not to address the question of the fetus's status.

Though the unsigned unanimous opinion reached the proper conclusion, it did so in a manner and in a context that makes it proper to label the opinion an instance of judicial activism. In the first place, if *Borowski* was moot, it is difficult to see why *Daigle* was not as well. Both cases were capable of laying down general rules for the nation. It is possible to think that in *Daigle* the Court exercised its discretion to find the case not moot because it wanted to validate the pro-abortion position and not the anti-abortion view.

The argument in *Borowski* that the legislature was not considering the protection of the fetus certainly seems correct, but it is equally applicable to the claimed right of a woman to an abortion. The two conclusions seem inseparable. Indeed, it may have been stronger in *Daigle*, since the omission of any position about abortion was known to have been deliberate in the framing of the *Charter of Rights*. The Canadian Court should have decided that neither the national nor the provincial *Charter* had anything at all to say about abortion – meaning that the Court had no authority to decide the case either way. The same conclusion should have been reached in the United States, where neither the Fifth nor the Fourteenth Amendment was ratified with any thought of abortion. In both countries, such rulings would have returned the moral issue of abortion to the legislatures, where the decision belongs. In both countries, the Justices elected to decide themselves what morality required.

In explaining his vote in the *Morgentaler* case, Chief Justice Lamer said in a 1997 interview that, while he was personally opposed to abortion, he even more firmly believed that he "should not impose upon others [his] personal beliefs." That statement can only mean that he is willing to impose on anti-abortionists the personal beliefs of those who favor abortion. Not only does the "explanation" leave the mystery of his vote murkier than ever but the statement is precisely the same as the lame excuse used by United States politicians who try to mollify both sides after voting for abortion: "I am personally opposed, but..." The Canadian Chief Justice thought the issue was his morality versus others' morality, though neither had been enacted in law. That approach can only be a surrender to New Class attitudes.

The Supreme Court's conduct in cases that in some way suggest that an unborn child is anything other than part of the mother's body is in striking contrast to the performance of the Court in creating laws favorable to

abortion. The slightest recognition of the fetus as a separate being threatens not only the legal but the moral
legitimacy of abortion. In these areas the Court adopts
the radical feminist position.

Winnipeg Child and Family Services v. *D.F.G.* (1997),
for example, reviewed a court order placing a woman in
the custody of the director of the agency until the birth
of her child. The woman had three previous children, two
of whom were permanently disabled because of her
addiction to glue sniffing. The case was moot by the time
it reached the Supreme Court, but the legal issues had
not previously been decided, so the Court proceeded to
decide the law in the abstract. The existing law of tort
was held not to support the order, and the question
become whether the common law should be extended
for that purpose. Here the Court showed a high degree
of modesty and respect for the legislature, which would
have been wholly admirable were it not in stark contrast
to its behavior where radical feminist views are opposed
to the legislature's choice. Justice McLachlin repeatedly
fell back on "the long-established principle that in a constitutional democracy it is the legislature, as the elected
branch of government, which should assume the major
responsibility for law reform." Quite true, but not at all
the way the Court behaved when it created homosexual
and abortion rights. One is tempted to conclude that the
difference is political rather than legal, and that the Court
in these cases was enacting the New Class agenda, which,
of course, includes the radical feminist agenda.

The dissent by Justices Major and Sopinka disagreed:

"To the extent that a change in the law in the circumstances of this case is required, the much admired flexibility of the common law has proven adaptable enough over centuries to meet exigent circumstances as they arise. That flexibility is surely needed in this appeal."

Whether one agrees with the majority or the dissent about the wisdom of deferring to the legislature when a change in law is proposed, it is surely true that the Court majority appears to have inverted the principle of deference. The common law has been the arena of judicial innovation, subject to the superior power of the legislature to revise the results. A constitution is, in contrast, even with the Canadian notwithstanding clause, almost immune to legislative revision. If judicial innovation is ever justifiable, therefore, it would appear to be so with respect to common law and not to constitutional law.

Homosexuality

Judicial normalization of homosexuality against the wishes of a majority of the electorate has gone much further in Canada than it has in the United States. When the *Charter* was being drafted, the government and the Parliamentary Committee on the Constitution refused to place protection for sexual orientation in the *Charter*, despite persistent lobbying by homosexual activist groups. Undeterred, in *Egan and Nesbitt* v. *Canada* (1995), the Supreme Court itself inserted sexual orientation as a forbidden ground of discrimination, along with race, national or ethnic origin, color, religion, sex, age, and physical or mental disability – grounds that the *Charter* makers did include in section 15, the equality provision. In the face of the *Charter's* silence – which was deliberate, indicating a desire to leave matters where they stood – the decision can only be called extraordinary. But what happened next may be viewed as requiring a stronger adjective.

The discussion that followed held it unconstitutional not to include sexual orientation as protected from discrimination in the Alberta Human Rights Act (*Vriend* v. *Alberta,* 1998) and as requiring spousal support on the dissolution of a homosexual relationship (*M.* v. *H.*, 1999). Segments of the homosexual rights movement are not satisfied with piecemeal reforms of this type. Their objective is to remake society so that homosexuality is regarded as the moral equivalent of heterosexuality. Since marriage has been defined as the union of a man and a woman, it follows that traditional understandings of marriage and the family must be undermined. Demanding the legalization and social recognition of same-sex marriages is a long step in that direction, and litigation is pending in lower Canadian courts to make such marriages a constitutional right (even as some American state courts have done). The equation of marriage between homosexuals and marriage between men and women was one result that voters and elected representatives were unwilling to reach.

Vriend is worth a closer look. In this case, when Delwin Vriend answered his employer, a private school, that he was gay, he was fired. A unanimous Supreme Court held that Alberta acted unconstitutionally in failing to include homosexuals in the list of groups specially protected from even private discrimination. Alberta's omission was deliberate because the subject was contentious and the public was roughly evenly divided. Justice Cory's opinion rejected the argument that courts should defer to the legislature's decision not to enact a particular provision because, among other things, it rested on "the very problematic distinction it draws between legislative action and inaction." Taken seriously, as one supposes it must be, that statement would mean that the Court can direct a legislature to act (which, together with the power to strike down enactments, would eliminate any need for a legislature) or, at the very least, it means that when the legislature deals with a topic, the Court can add such amendments as it thinks should have been included. It is a remarkable assertion of judicial supremacy. The Court said the democratic process had not responded adequately (there could, apparently, be only one adequate response). Overriding the legislature, the Court required that the province's *Individual Rights Protection Act* be enforced as though it contained protection for homosexuals. This decision was an astounding judicial intrusion based on a bizarre rationale. The Court made it clear that it was assuming the role of the ultimate arbiter of the "democratic values and principles" of the *Charter*. The result was a dramatic invasion of the legislature's domain. Significantly, the Alberta legislature did not respond by invoking the notwithstanding clause to undo the Court's adventurism. Rather, it promised to use section 33 to negate any court rulings imposing same-sex marriages. By then, the notwithstanding clause had become virtually illegitimate in the view of many, and, in any case, a legislature too divided to enact a measure cannot muster the votes to repeal the Court's decision.

In *M. v. H.* (1999) the Supreme Court, by a vote of eight to one, held that denying same-sex couples access to Ontario's spousal support legislation violated the guarantee of equality without discrimination. Justices Cory and Iacobucci, writing for the Court, stated:

> The exclusion of same-sex partners...promotes the view that M., and individuals in same-sex relationships generally, are less worthy of recognition and protection. It implies that they are judged to be incapable of forming intimate relationships of economic independence [or was it dependence?] as compared to opposite-sex couples.... [S]uch exclusion perpetuates the disadvantages suffered by individuals in same-sex relationships and contributes to the erasure of their existence.

Lower courts have overturned definitions of "spouse" that exclude members of same-sex partnerships; required that members of same-sex couples be allowed jointly to adopt children; and held that a benefits statute could not contain a separate definition of "same-sex partner" and opposite-sex partner, even though both received the same benefits, because the separate definitions create a separate regime that separates (though only verbally) members of the two kinds of partnerships.

As Justice Claire L'Heureux-Dubé said in her notes

for an address at an international conference on how to normalize homosexuality: "Changes in the legal realm, however, have been accompanied by a general failure of the political process to recognize the rights of lesbians and gays without the pressure of court decisions behind them." Attempts to make changes through the political process, she said, have been controversial and have often led to public criticism and backlash. She then cited changing public opinion polls on these subjects to show that the public is generally supportive of extending rights to same-sex couples. "This indicates that courts are taking the lead in changing society's attitudes to same-sex partnerships." After that statement, it must have taken considerable courage to assert that court judgments in this area "reflect the values of ordinary Canadians."

Substantive Due Process in the Guise of "Fundamental Justice"

The Canadian Court has even reproduced, under another name, and against the intentions of the *Charter*'s drafters, the American excrescence of substantive due process. *British Columbia Motor Vehicle Reference* (1985) concerned the constitutionality of a provision in the province's *Motor Vehicle Act* which made the act of driving with a suspended license an absolute liability defense (one not dependent on criminal intent) punishable by mandatory imprisonment and a fine. The Court faced the question of whether section 7 of the *Charter* – guaranteeing the right not to be deprived of life, liberty, or security of the person except in accordance with the principles of fundamental justice – was to be given a substantive or a procedural meaning. That is, was the Court confined to judging the fairness of the procedure by which the law was applied or could it also judge the appropriateness of the law's substantive content? This, of course, was the same question the United States Supreme Court faced – and answered so disastrously in *Dred Scott* – in construing the due process clause's guarantee of the same rights. "There was," Knopff and Morton note, "ample documentary evidence that many of the most influential framers intended the narrower, procedural meaning."

Manfredi makes it clear just how strong that evidence was. The draft of section 7 used the phrase "due process of law." But those words were objected to on the grounds that the Canadian courts could use them, as the American courts had, to develop a doctrine of substantive due process allowing the courts themselves to judge the substance of the law for reasonableness. The language change was made in response to that objection. "To the officials of the Justice Department responsible for drafting the Charter . . . the phrase 'principles of fundamental justice' . . . did not have any substantive connotation in Canadian law. . . ." A representative of the department, in testimony before the Special Joint Committee on the Constitution in 1981, stated:

> [T]he words "fundamental justice" would cover the same thing as what is called procedural due process, that is the meaning of due process in

relation to requiring fair procedure. However, it in our view does not cover the concept of what is called substantive due process, which would impose substantive requirements as to the policy of the law in question.

Minister of Justice Jean Chrétien reported the same understanding to the committee.

The clarity of this history did not deter Justice Lamer, who reached a conclusion that Manfredi, with considerable restraint, calls "remarkable." The clear intention of the legislature did not save the Act from a declaration of unconstitutionality. The Justice discounted the testimony of the Justice Department and the minister of justice because it was given by civil servants and did not sufficiently indicate the intentions of the legislative bodies that adopted the *Charter*. The absence of any counterargument in those bodies would normally, of course, indicate that they agreed with the drafters. If the Court bound itself to the substantive intent underlying the various constitutional guarantees, the *Charter*'s rights and freedoms would "become frozen in time to the moment of adoption, with little or no possibility of growth and adjustment to changing societal needs." This interpretation, of course, ignores the function of Parliament and the provincial legislatures in meeting changing societal needs.

Some Canadian commentators see the same problems that certain of their United States counterparts do with judicial review. Manfredi agreed that "rights-based judicial review is a positive element of liberal democracy" because it safeguards "individual rights and liberties by enforcing constitutional limits on legislative and executive power," ensuring that "liberal democracy does not degenerate into tyranny." But he went on in a passage partially quoted in the epigraph to this chapter:

> On the other hand, rights-based judicial review taken to its extreme becomes an anti-democratic power, wielded by courts to alter the fundamental character of a nation's constitution without significant popular participation or even public awareness. Left unchecked, judicial power in this sense poses the same threat to liberal democracy as do other forms and uses of political power.... [In Canada] judicial power has continued to expand as the legitimacy of the notwithstanding clause has been further eroded. Judicial supremacy, in other words, is overtaking constitutional supremacy.

Justice Lamer, among others, undeterred by the fact that the *Charter* was meant to deny the Court an unstructured authority to judge the substance of statutes in the guise of constitutional interpretation, used the "living tree" metaphor to justify rejecting the framers' original understanding of what it was they were doing in favor of the judicial understanding of what should be done now. The metaphor is both misleading and pernicious. Under the similar name of the "living Constitution," it serves the same illegitimate function in America as in Canada. A constitution necessarily grows when a judge applies existing principles to unforeseen circumstances. That is what Holmes meant when he said that the movements of the courts were properly molecular rather than molar. It is the task of today's judge to discern how the constitution makers' principles, defined in the world they knew, apply to the circumstances of the world the judges know. As I wrote some time ago, "The world changes in which unchanging values find their application."

Examples in American law are plentiful. I cited the Fourth Amendment's prohibition of unreasonable searches and seizures, written to prevent the constable, acting on nothing more solid than his own whim or vague suspicion, from entering upon a citizen's home. The amendment's general words, however, indicate a general principle, a presumption of privacy against unwarranted government intrusion in the name of law enforcement. After an initial hesitation, the Supreme Court applied the principle to modern technologies of electronic surveillance. More recently, the Court has applied the principle to police use of thermal imaging to detect certain activities within a home. The technique of judicial adaptation does not, of course, apply simply to changes in technology. In an opinion that ruffled some of my conservative colleagues on the bench, I applied the First Amendment guarantee of freedom of the press to defeat a libel claim. Granting that the framers of the amendment did not see libel actions as a threat to press freedom, I argued that, over time, if the libel action evolved so that in some of its new applications it became dangerous to that freedom, judges should properly adapt their doctrines to deal with the new problem. A change in the legal environment provided by common law or statutory law is surely no different from a constitutional judge's standpoint than is a change in the technological environment.

It is quite another thing, however, to say that the "living tree" metaphor means that judges must keep up with the times and with changing conditions by creating new constitutional principles to be enforced as if they were actually in the document. At that point the judiciary arrogates to itself the powers of a constitutional convention, with one difference: a constitution must be submitted to the people or their representatives for approval before it goes into effect; a judge's amendment to a constitution needs no imprimatur from anyone but the judge.

In a similar locution, a court's invention of a new principle – the right to an abortion, say, or the special protection of homosexuality – is often justified by saying that "our" understanding of an old value such as equality has evolved. The lie in that formulation is the word "our." If the new understanding of equality had evolved, that fact would be reflected in legislation – and, in fact, it often is, as demonstrated by civil rights statutes. But when judges make the supposed evolutionary change in understanding the basis for declaring a statute invalid, it is perfectly obvious that the change is not ours, but theirs. And in that they are speaking for the values of the New Class which have not yet found, and perhaps never can find, favor in the legislature.

Morton and Knopff conclude *The Charter Revolution and the Court Party* with an observation that applies not only to Canada but to activist courts everywhere:

To transfer the resolution of reasonable disagreement from legislatures to courts inflates rhetoric to unwarranted levels and replaces negotiated, majoritarian compromise policies with the intensely held policy preferences of minorities. Rights-based judicial policymaking also grants the policy preferences of courtroom victors an aura of coercive force and permanence that they do not deserve. Issues that should be subject to the ongoing flux of government by discussion are presented as beyond legitimate debate, with the partisans claiming the right to permanent victory. As the morality of rights displaces the morality of consent, the politics of coercion replaces the politics of persuasion. The result is to embitter politics and decrease the inclination of political opponents to treat each other as fellow citizens – that is, as members of a sovereign people.

3

ISRAEL

The autonomy of the individual . . . exists because it is recognized by the law.

The moment that a certain realm is not justiciable, the wielder of power does whatever he wants.

[The judge] must sometimes depart the confines of his legal system and channel into it fundamental values not yet found in it.

The world is filled with law.

Justice Aharon Barak,
president of the Supreme Court of Israel

Pride of place in the international judicial deformation of democratic government goes not to the United States, nor to Canada, but to the State of Israel. The Israeli Supreme Court[1] is making itself the dominant institution in the nation, an authority no other court in the world has achieved.

Imagine, if you can, a supreme court that has gained the power to choose its own members, wrested control of the attorney general from the executive branch, set aside legislation and executive action when there were disagreements about policy, altered the meaning of enacted law, forbidden government action at certain times, ordered action it thought the government should take at other times, and claimed and exercised the authority to override national defense measures. Imagine as well a supreme court that has created a body of constitutional law despite the absence of an actual constitution. No act of imagination is required: Israel's Supreme Court has done them all.

It was not always so. Though Israel has been a highly politicized nation from its formation, the Supreme Court, in order to establish its legitimacy, according to Martin Edelman, wrote opinions that were "characterized by highly formalistic legal style, narrow interpretations of

[1] *The Israeli Court sits as either the Supreme Court or as the High Court of Justice. The latter hears petitions for the redress of grievances brought against the government. It is a court of first instance, or original jurisdiction: cases are brought directly to it rather than coming up on appeal from lower courts. The distinction between Supreme Court and High Court is irrelevant to much of the discussion here and, for convenience, the text will often refer simply to the Supreme Court.*

statutes and precedents, adherence to *stare decisis*, and deference to the decisions of the Knesset, the government,
and the Israel Defense Forces." Gradually, however, the
Court began to assert its authority to interpret statutes
according to the principles of "natural justice" – an
amorphous concept designed to cut the Court loose
from the restraints of positive law. But the subjectivity
was too obvious. Searching for something that could be
designated a mandate for overriding judicial power, the
Supreme Court began to claim that its supremacy had
been legitimated in 1992 by the passage of two laws: the
Basic Law: Freedom of Occupation and the *Basic Law:
Human Dignity and Liberty*. The first of these laws forbids
restrictions on the right to practice any vocation. The
second, which is more important for our purposes, prohibits infringements on a person's dignity, life, body, or
property. Each *Basic Law* contains an exception clause:
"There shall be no violation of rights under this Basic
Law except by a law befitting the values of the State of
Israel, enacted for a proper purpose, and to an extent no
greater than is required." An earlier clause in both laws
describes Israel's values as those of a "Jewish and democratic state."[2] These words seem at least marginally more
confining than "natural justice," but in practice they have
liberated rather than constrained the Court.

These *Basic Laws* provide an inadequate platform for a

---

[2]   *The* Basic Law *follows the pattern of the* Canadian Charter of Rights
and Freedoms, *stating rights in unqualified language and then, since
government would be impossible if all rights were absolute, stating the
conditions on which the rights may be limited.*

Court intent on invalidating legislative action. For one thing, the *Basic Laws* are even more general and undefined than major provisions in the United States *Bill of Rights* and the *Canadian Charter of Rights and Freedoms*. The American amendments and the Canadian *Charter* were, at least, written, proposed, and ratified as constitutions. By contrast, it is not at all clear that Israel's *Basic Laws* were designed to be more than precatory. The *Basic Laws* were enacted by the Knesset in the middle of the night without even a majority of the 120 members present. The *Law* dealing with liberty and dignity passed by 32 to 21 votes; that dealing with freedom of occupation by 23 to 0. There was no discussion in the Knesset indicating any recognition that a constitution was being adopted. Certainly there was no understanding that the Supreme Court was to be the final arbiter of what the *Basic Laws* meant. Yet that is how the Court has chosen to read them.

The extraordinary events that followed cannot be understood without reference to one man, Aharon Barak. From the beginning of his tenure on the Supreme Court in 1978 to his assumption of the presidency in 1995 to the present day, Barak has been the dominant figure in Israeli law and, increasingly, a major force in shaping the nation's policies. He is without significant opposition within the Court. So broadly has he spread the Court's powers that it is no exaggeration to say, along with Hillel Neuer, that "Barak may well be the single most influential person in Israeli public life today." Barak's philosophy, now apparently shared by the Court, is that there is no area of Israeli life that the Court may not rule. This radical position follows from three extraordinary legal doctrines also adopted by the Canadian Supreme Court, whose *Charter* jurisprudence has greatly influenced the Israeli Court. But these doctrines appear to have led in Israel to an even more extreme body of decisions than Canada's, or any other nation's for that matter: first, all behavior, governmental or personal, is examinable and may be controlled by the Court; second, all persons may raise any issues they choose for consideration by the Court; and third, all questions are fit for Court resolution. These are not dusty technicalities, but revolutionary changes in the Court's role in government and, hence, in the distribution of power within Israel.

The first doctrine holds that since law covers everything, even those areas on which the law is silent, freedom from law is a legal issue reviewable by the Court. Since nothing escapes the legal maw, Israel may not allow freedoms of which its Court disapproves. "Constitutional law" about private behavior, therefore, may be devised without the benefit of a constitution. By contrast, in the United States there must be action by government, usually in the form of a legal command, to trigger constitutional scrutiny.

The second doctrine, standing, holds that parties may address a court only if they allege injuries to themselves which the court has the authority to redress. A mere personal or ideological disagreement with government is not enough. President Barak and his Court have done away with that limitation on their power. Anybody who thinks the government is misbehaving in some respect can litigate, even if the alleged misbehavior affects him not at all.

Thus, a citizen with a private grievance against a Cabinet appointee can litigate the worthiness of this person on grounds having nothing to do with any specific injury to the complainant. It is as though a United States citizen, unharmed by an action of the Federal Reserve Board, could go to the U.S. Supreme Court to litigate the wisdom of an interest rate hike.

The doctrine of justiciability, the third on the list, requires that the issues to be litigated must be fit for courts to decide. Barak has reshaped the law so that practically any subject, no matter how political, may be decided by the Court. The issue may be legal or simply one that the Court considers in the public interest. Virtually every subject, then, is justiciable. Barak sees two categories of justiciability – one normative and the other institutional – though he and the Court have little use for any restriction that might arise from such categorization. Normative justiciability raises the question whether legal criteria exist which a court can apply in the case proffered to it. If there are no such criteria, the matter is not one for judicial resolution. Institutional justiciability raises the question whether the subject matter is appropriate for judicial decision or whether some other branch of government may more properly decide the issue.

Normative nonjusticiability is inconceivable in Barak's world view because no legal void can exist: law covers everything. Legal criteria – which mean no more than the Court's willingness to decide – always exist. Even an activity bearing the greatest political character, such as the making of war or peace, is examinable by judicial criteria.

The decision whether to intervene or not, however, lies entirely within the Court's discretion. Institutional justiciability is similarly toothless because, should the Court say that an issue is committed to another branch of government and inappropriate for judicial intervention, the Court essentially grants the government freedom to behave illegally. That is not to be tolerated. The Court, of course, cannot behave illegally, since it is the law.

The extremes to which Barak's judicial philosophy can carry him is shown by his statement that the deployment of troops in wartime is a justiciable issue. Barak recognizes, however, that the public may not want the Court deciding certain issues. In highly political cases, therefore, such as that involving the Oslo peace process, Barak and the majority of the Court chose to limit universal justiciability and not to intervene directly. A second exception to universal justiciability arises in cases where justice may not seem to be done, but Court action itself would undermine public confidence in the judiciary. These exceptions clearly overlap, if they are not identical. In both instances, however, the Court's power is not limited by principle, but only by fear of adverse public reaction. This justification denotes concern for the prestige of the Court, not for the integrity of the law or the vitality of democracy.

A comparison with the activist American Supreme Court demonstrates how far the Israeli Supreme Court has gone. The American Court does not hold that law is everywhere. With the sole exception of the Thirteenth Amendment, which bans involuntary servitude (any condition approaching that of slavery), the American

Constitution applies only to action taken by the state, not to its inaction. Although the Court has strained to find state action in cases of racial discrimination, it remains true that most private behavior is beyond the reach of the Court's constitutional power and must be regulated, if at all, according to laws made by elected representatives in the legislatures.

In the United States, the doctrine of standing has, as its constitutional core, the requirement that the plaintiff must have suffered an "injury in fact" – an invasion of a legally protected interest that is concrete, particularized, and either actual or imminent. It cannot be merely conjectural or hypothetical. An American federal court could not, for example, entertain a citizen's lawsuit complaining that a Cabinet member was not fit for her position. The Court has held that taxpayers and citizens lacked standing to sue on the claim that the Constitution required the CIA's budget to be published, or that members of Congress are constitutionally disqualified from holding reserve commissions in the armed forces. By comparison, when members of a citizens' rights movement challenged the Israeli justice minister's refusal to extradite a person wanted for murder abroad, the majority of the Court asserted a new standard by holding that the petition could be reviewed by the Court. The Justices said that, because it was a matter of genuine public concern and no one else in the country had a more direct interest in the case, the Court would hear the petition.

The Israeli Court's power is further magnified by the ability of litigants complaining about the government to proceed directly to the Supreme Court, rather than reaching that tribunal after trial and appeal in lower courts. U.S. law about justiciability derives from the separation of the powers of the three branches of government. A court will stay its hand, according to *Baker* v. *Carr* (1961), for several reasons: a textually demonstrable constitutional commitment of the issue to another branch of government; a lack of judicially discoverable and manageable standards for resolving a dispute; an inability to decide without a determination of policy that is clearly of nonjudicial discretion; an inability for the court to decide the case without expressing a lack of respect due to coordinate branches of government; an unusual need for unquestioning adherence to a political decision already made; or the potential for embarrassment from multifarious pronouncements by various departments on one question.

The American Court applies these concepts of state action, standing, and justiciability to confine its own power. These self-limiting doctrines are, of course, more complex than a brief statement can indicate, but the nub of the matter is clear: these boundaries on judicial power assist in preserving legislative power and democratic authority.

In addition to this astonishing array of judicial powers, the selection process for the Israeli Court's Justices, established in 1953, ensures, as Mordechai Haller says, that "in Israel the judiciary selects itself." The choice of a Justice is made by a Judicial Selections Committee composed of the president of the Supreme Court, two other Justices chosen by that Court, the justice minister, an additional minister appointed by the government, two members of the Knesset, and two members of the Israeli Bar Association.

That makeup, according to Haller, ensures that the influence of the Justices is "nearly absolute" and "it is almost unheard of that a nominee to the high court would be either approved or rejected over the objections of the justices on the committee." Quite naturally, the Justices prefer candidates with views similar to their own. The result is a Court without serious internal dissension or debate, a Court that agrees with and is led by Aharon Barak.

The activist decisions of the Supreme Court of Israel fall into two categories. The first comprises interventions in the internal operations of the other branches of government. These decisions have been extraordinarily intrusive, perhaps reflecting the belief that the Knesset and the executive are not trustworthy. The second includes rulings on human rights. These decisions display a willingness to substitute the Court's own extremely liberal New Class values for the moral and prudent choices made by democratic institutions. The Court's values implement a socialist impulse in cultural and social affairs: they are universalistic in scope and, to the exclusion of competing values, stress such concerns as the dignity, freedom, and equality of individuals. As rhetoric, those words are highly persuasive; as operational concepts, they have often proved highly deleterious.

Interference with the Workings of Government
The Court's activism became undisguised imperialism when, in a bold and unprecedented stroke, it revolutionalized the internal structure of government – and the

distribution of governmental power – by anointing the attorney general as the supreme authority within the executive branch. In the 1993 *Pinhasi* case (*Amitai-Citizens for Good Government and Integrity* v. *The Prime Minister of Israel*) the issue was whether Deputy Religious Affairs Minister Rafael Pinhasi had to resign when he was indicted for tax and party-funding violations. Prime Minister Yitzhak Rabin would not fire Pinhasi because that would endanger the thin parliamentary majority in favor of the Oslo accords. The attorney general, who had sole authority to represent the government in litigation, announced that he would not defend Rabin's decision. The Court went beyond the legal merits of the case to announce that the government (though not the Court) was bound by the attorney general's decision – effectively converting that officer into a judge dominating the executive branch from within.

Perhaps not surprisingly, jurists proclaimed the Court's decision a victory for the rule of law. It is difficult to understand, however, why making a subordinate government official the arbiter of the government's actions, responsible only to his own sense of discretion, is not the antithesis of the rule of law. The government may have quite respectable legal arguments opposed to the attorney general's view, but those views cannot be heard by the Court and are set at naught. Still worse, an attorney general's decision is effectively final even when it is not based in law but is a conclusion about policy. "In Israel, with the world's most liberal rules of standing and justiciability," Jonathan Rosenblum noted, "the only party that cannot get a ruling on the legality of governmental action is the government itself, if the Attorney General refuses to defend the government's position."

Pinhasi was the culmination of a series of aggrandizements by which successive attorneys general expanded the powers of the office. Foremost among them was none other than Aharon Barak, who later wrote the *Pinhasi* opinion when he was on the Court. His prosecution of numerous powerful figures in the Labor Party, including the wife of the prime minister, "did much to cultivate the idea that only a truly independent attorney general, free of any political concerns, could effectively combat corruption in high office," according to Evelyn Gordon.[3] In the process, however, independent Israeli attorneys general have committed a series of outrages, or what other democracies would consider outrages.

Attorneys general have, for example, objected to independent telecommunications and postal authorities, not on legal, but on economic grounds; conducted a vitriolic campaign against a new Knesset faction and its leader; and judged the propriety of political compromises essential to the formation of coalition governments not on the ground that they were illegal, but merely because, in the

---

[3] *In the United States, a similar sentiment led to the creation of the Office of the Independent Counsel, charged with investigating and, if warranted, prosecuting high executive branch officials. Like Israel's attorney general, the independent counsel was accountable to no elected official. The innovation proved unsatisfactory to both political parties, particularly when the executive of their own party was subjected to the independent counsel's ministrations. The office has been allowed to lapse unmourned.*

opinion of the attorney general, the compromises were "inappropriate." A man was denied the position of minister of public security because the attorney general said an indictment for violation of privacy disqualified the applicant from holding any position with access to sensitive personal information. The fact that, as a member of the special "security cabinet," he had access to all classified documents, in any event, was ignored. He was acquitted, but too late to reverse his disqualification. As Evelyn Gordon justly said: "With the alacrity of a seasoned despot, [the attorney general] managed to take his own, wholly unlegislated notions of political propriety, translate them into a legal presumption of guilt without trial, and impose them on the composition of government without having to convince *anyone* he was right – handing a major setback to the innocent [man] and the tens of thousands of voters who had found voice in his party."

The full extent of the abuse to which the powers of the attorney general lend themselves was disclosed when Prime Minister Netanyahu named Ya'akov Ne'eman as justice minister. A petitioner hostile to Ne'eman accused him of a number of crimes, most of which had already been investigated and found baseless. Though Ne'eman was initially investigated on a charge of suborning a witness, the prosecution found insufficient evidence to bring a case. But simultaneous with its announcement that there would be no indictment for subornation, the prosecution announced that suspicion remained and that Ne'eman would be indicted instead for perjury and obstruction of justice for his conduct during the subornation investigation. The evidence for that charge was trivial mistakes about such things as dates in his affidavit, anomalies he discovered himself and corrected. Some months later Ne'eman was acquitted in court, but he had already had to resign because of the attorney general's charges. Gordon remarks: "The mindboggling assertion that the role of the nation's top law enforcement officials includes besmirching public officials whom they fail to indict – an assumption that met with virtually no public opposition – speaks volumes not only about the tendentiousness of [the law enforcement officials] but also about a poisonous admixture of the legal and moral responsibilities that the public has come to expect in the attorney-general." Similarly, when the attorney general found there was not enough evidence to indict either Prime Minister Netanyahu or Justice Minister Hanegbi, he issued a report that there was nevertheless "real suspicion" that Netanyahu was, in fact, guilty.[4]

The powers the Court has lodged in the attorney general can hardly be overestimated. *The Movement for Quality Government in Israel* v. *Prime Minister Ariel Sharon*

---

[4] *The U.S. Office of the Independent Counsel was similarly an invitation to political abuse; some independent counsel resisted the temptation; others embraced it. One counsel, for example, filed a written report stating that, though he declined to indict, he believed a nominee to the post of attorney general had violated the law. Another probably influenced the choice of a president when, just days before the election, he filed an indictment of an official which noted, gratuitously, that he thought George Bush, the incumbent president, knew more than he admitted about supposed illegalities.*

(2001) arose from Attorney General Elyakim Rubinstein's ruling that Sharon could not use his son, Omri, as an emissary to Yasser Arafat. Although Omri was not to be paid, Rubinstein said it was nepotistic, not in accord with the norms of good government, and therefore impermissible. He qualified that by saying Omri could be used if it were really a "life-or-death" situation. Ignoring the ruling, Sharon continued to use Omri, saying that, in Israel's situation, all such missions are potentially life or death. The Movement for Quality Government went to the Court, arguing that Sharon was breaking the law by violating Rubinstein's directive. After a few hearings, Sharon surrendered and told the Court that though he thought Rubenstein wrong in principle, he would not use Omri without Rubenstein's permission. Rubinstein replied that if he received such a request, he would consult with various security and defense officials before giving or denying consent. The unelected attorney general, rather than the elected prime minister, now decides when a life-or-death situation exists and when it does not.

The prime minister was further hamstrung when the Court, in denying a new government the power to replace the civil service commissioner, announced a rationale that, at the very least, strongly suggests that a new government may not replace the attorney general, and hence that no attorney general may be dismissed at any time. Even the government's authority to choose an attorney general when the post becomes vacant may be put in question. Bills were drawn up by both the Netanyahu and the Barak governments which stated that the government must submit its proposed candidates for attorney general to a five-member committee that could propose its own candidates. The committee's choice would be referred to the Cabinet, which could approve or reject the nominee. The committee, headed by a retired Supreme Court Justice, would be composed, additionally, of a former justice minister or attorney general appointed by the Cabinet, a member of the Knesset chosen by the Knesset Constitution Committee, an attorney chosen by the Bar Association, and an academic chosen by the deans of Israel's law schools. The committee could reject any candidate it considered "improper," a term that meant having personal or political ties to someone in the government. That process severely undercuts the government's ability to choose someone known to be sympathetic to its agenda. Owing to changes in the Knesset, these bills were never enacted. They reflect, however, the widespread opinion, perhaps influenced by the Supreme Court's decisions, that the attorney general should play a role independent of, and even contradictory to, the elected government's policies.

Even without these proposals, as Gordon makes plain, "the reality is grim enough. The government is now saddled with a senior official who has the legal authority to veto virtually any government action or policy, against whom it has no means of appeal, and of whom it can rid itself only with the utmost difficulty, if at all; and with an outside committee which has the power to veto any candidate who would be too likely to use his power in line with the government's wishes." It is extraordinary that the Israeli public should accept the idea of an attorney general capable of hamstringing the executive branch that the public votes into office. There would seem to be less and less reason for the Israeli people to bother electing a legislature and executive; the attorney general, with the backing of the Supreme Court, can decide almost everything for them. "Replacing the normal methods of democratic oversight with the oversight of a single, all-powerful unelected official," Gordon concludes, "is not entirely different from replacing democracy with autocracy." If the Court is added to that summation, democracy is actually slowly being replaced by oligarchy.

The Supreme Court has adopted a standard of reasonableness for judging government decisions and actions. As a result, the range of decisions that could potentially be overturned became almost identical with the totality of government action. The Court has dramatically increased its involvement in the day-to-day governance of the country and, in recent years, has ruled on governmental decisions and actions that, in the past, were denied review. The issue of compulsory army service provides an example. After the defense minister exempted full-time yeshiva students from compulsory army service, there were a series of challenges to the law. In 1981 the Court ruled that the issue was not justiciable. In 1986 it ruled that it was justiciable, but that the exemption was a reasonable exercise of the minister's authority. In 1998, however, in *Amnon Rubenstein* v. *Minister of Defense*, the Court decided that the exemption was unreasonable because the number of yeshiva students had increased. This ruling substituted the Court's discretion for the discretion the Knesset had lodged in the defense minister. The Court was now deciding how many exemptions defense policy could afford. It deferred implementation for one year to give the Knesset time to enact legislation, and then granted additional extensions. The Knesset ultimately legislated a further two-year continuation of the exemptions while it considers the issue. In response to a petition that this extension be held unconstitutional, the Court created an eleven-Justice panel to consider the issue, but no ruling has yet been handed down.

The Court's self-arrogated authority to overturn government decisions solely on the Court's judgment that the action in question is "unreasonable" was again displayed when the Transport Ministry's traffic supervisor, who is legally authorized to close major roads, decided to close a street that the Haredi (ultra-Orthodox Jews) wanted closed on the Sabbath. The Court recommended that the government appoint a commission to study the issue, which the government did. But the commission agreed with the closing. The Court then resumed hearings and prohibited the closure. The Justices cited no law or right that had been violated, but simply thought it unreasonable and, therefore, illegal.

The reasonability standard disregards the separation of powers. In judging reasonableness, the Court necessarily replaces the legislative process. It claims that it uses the power to overturn unreasonable government decisions only where the decisions are so egregious that "it is inconceivable that any reasonable authority would be

likely to make [them]" – which must mean that a majority of otherwise sensible people are behaving so irra-
tionally as to approach temporary insanity. But the cases in
which the power has been used show that the standard of
unreasonableness is much lower than the Court suggests
and amounts to no more than second-guessing. The Israeli
Supreme Court's standard of "reasonableness" is equivalent to the United States Supreme Court's "substantive
due process" and the Canadian Supreme Court's "fundamental justice." All these terms are formulations of the
judiciary's never-ending quest for a form of words that
will justify judicial power that is essentially lawless. The
three formulas differ in only one respect: the American
and Canadian Courts perverted the plain meaning of
procedural guarantees in order to seize an authority over
the substance of legislation, while the Israeli Court simply
imported an innocuous-sounding standard to achieve the
same radical assumption of illegitimate power.

The Court has vetoed the Cabinet's choice for director general of a government ministry, overturned the
Knesset decision to lift the parliamentary immunity of a
member of the Knesset so he could stand trial, and
denied the government's right to continue a fifty-
year-old ban on the import of nonkosher meat. It has
overturned the attorney general's decision not to try certain public figures, prevented the government from
dismissing its civil service commissioner, and even overturned the Israel Prize Committee's choice of a prize
recipient. In *Raphael Pinhasi* v. *Knesset of Israel* (1993) the
Court overturned the Knesset's decision to lift Pinhasi's

parliamentary immunity so he would stand trial for violations of tax and party-funding laws on the ground that the Knesset was playing a "quasi-judicial" role and had not met standards of judicial fairness. Members had not, for example, been given copies of the indictment or had enough time to read the protocols of the House Committee's lengthy analysis of the issue. The quasi-judicial rationale was preposterous because the Knesset did not try or convict Pinhasi of any offense, but merely gave permission for him to stand trial, where he would have been entitled to full procedural regularity.

There appear to be few limits to the Supreme Court's willingness to interfere in political matters. In *Yosef Zberzhevsky* v. *Prime Minister* (1990) the Court overturned a coalition agreement between the Likud and a small faction in which the Likud agreed to cancel a debt that the smaller party owed it. The Court said that this agreement was equivalent to buying power and therefore illegal. In *Ze'ev Welner* v. *Chairman of the Labor Party* (1994) Labor and Shas agreed that, "If the status quo in religious affairs is violated [by a decision of the Supreme Court], the two sides promise to correct the violation by means of appropriate legislation." The attorney general declared the agreement "inappropriate, and not to be acted upon." During initial hearings, the Justices made it clear they were likely to rule the same way. Labor and Shas then altered the wording: "In any case where the two sides think the status quo has been violated, the two sides will investigate, in a serious and reasonable manner – considering each case on its own merits – how it is possible to restore the status quo, and will act accordingly...If it becomes clear that the only way to restore the status quo is through legislation, the two sides will use their discretion as to the appropriate content of such legislation." Labor promised Shas that this wording meant the same thing as the previous form of the agreement. It must have taken some acrobatic lawyering to produce the identical promise disguised in verbose prose. Even so, the agreement slipped by the Court by only a 3 to 2 vote.

Interference with National Security

In assessing the Supreme Court's performance in the area of national security, it is essential to remember the nation's extremely precarious position in the Middle East. All the nations surrounding Israel ardently desire the country's destruction and, indeed, the annihilation of the Jews. Arab terrorist organizations regularly commit bloody outrages against the civilian population. A major portion of Israeli citizens are Arabs, some of whom are of dubious loyalty. Considering the dangers continually confronting Israel, its responses to terrorist attacks and the threat of invasion have been quite moderate, sometimes arguably too moderate. Be that as it may, one would suppose that the nation's courts would stay out of life-and-death decisions about national security and defense. Yet the opposite has been the case.

The Court suggested in *Committee Against Torture* v. *Government of Israel* (2000) that it may take over the supervision of the methods of interrogation employed by

Israel's General Security Service against suspected terrorists. The GSS had been using both psychological and physical techniques, such as shaking, sleep deprivation, and placing those waiting for interrogation in the "Shabach" position (the prisoner seated on a low chair tilted forward, hands tied uncomfortably behind his back, head covered by an opaque sack, all while powerfully loud music was played in the room). Although very unpleasant and potentially damaging, these techniques did not come close in severity to those used by many other security forces around the world. The GSS's decision to use physical force in each case was based on internal regulations that required permission from various ranks in the GSS hierarchy and that were themselves approved by a special Ministerial Committee. President Barak's opinion for the Court acknowledged Isreal's extremely perilous situation, which "has been engaged in an unceasing struggle for both its very existence and security, from the day of its founding." The difficulty was that the *Basic Law: Human Dignity and Liberty* contains clauses guaranteeing freedom from violation of a person's body or dignity and from restrictions of liberty by imprisonment. The rights could be violated only "by a law befitting the values of the State of Israel, enacted for a proper purpose, and to an extent no greater than is required." But the Knesset had never passed legislation authorizing GSS interrogation techniques or even authorizing the existence of the GSS. The Court's decision disapproving of the techniques was, therefore, correct, but the rhetoric was so disapproving that any legislation authorizing the GSS's techniques would very probably be very unlikely to pass the Court's interpretation of values, proper purpose, and least-restrictive means. An additional problem is that the decision to use force and the degree necessary will always depend on the facts of a particular case. It is difficult to see how the Knesset can do more than articulate general principles, and even then the Court may well disapprove of their application.[5]

Terrorist organizations, often in cooperation with Arab governments, seize and hold Israeli soldiers hostage. Israel's Defense Force retaliates in a variety of ways, among them by holding terrorists in order to assist negotiations leading to an exchange of prisoners. In *John Doe* v. *Minister of Defense* (2000) the Supreme Court of Israel ruled that the IDF had to release eight Lebanese prisoners, members of the Hizballah, it had held past the expiration of their prison terms as leverage in securing the release of Israeli prisoners of war. In a 6 to 3 vote, President Barak, writing for the majority, ordered the Lebanese prisoners set free. No law prevented the IDF from using this "bargaining chip" tactic, but Barak wrote that holding the guerrillas violated their dignity and freedom. An important means of preserving national security was taken away by the Court.

---

5   *The United States has addressed a similar difficulty with respect to electronic surveillance in national security cases by creating a special court, whose proceedings are secret, to grant or deny applications for warrants to conduct such surveillance. Though this is not, and for obvious reasons, cannot be an adversarial proceeding, it does provide supervision by an independent judiciary that can take into account in advance the particular facts of each case.*

These cases do not stand alone. *Kedan* v. *Israel Lands Administration* (2000), known as the *Katzir* decision after the community involved, held that the government could not refuse Arab citizens of Israel the right to establish residence in Katzir, which was situated along with seven other communities to create a buffer zone against areas with large Arab populations. The admission of Arabs, citizens of Israel or not, to such communities would endanger and perhaps defeat the defensive purpose of the bufferzone policy. Barak wrote the opinion holding that use of the criteria of nationality or religion was discrimination and, therefore, a violation of the principle of equality. The disingenuity of the reasoning need not detain us. The important point is that, once again, universalistic principles were deployed to harm Israel's security, without adequately weighing Israel's particular circumstance and needs.

These three cases indicate the direction in which the Court is headed. Perhaps the Israeli public should begin to take seriously President Barak's assertion that the Court has the authority to rule on the deployment of military forces in wartime.

Homosexuality

The Supreme Court has been active in normalizing homosexual conduct. Given its absorption with abstract versions of equality, freedom, and dignity, it could hardly be otherwise. Still, the decision in *Berner-Kadish* v. *Minister of Interior* (2000) must have come as a shock: the

Court's protectiveness of homosexual relations in this case led it to redefine the family unit. A lesbian couple asked that both of them be registered as the mother of a boy whom one had borne and the other adopted under California law. (California has a peculiar culture. Americans have a saying that the continent is tilted and that everything loose rolls to the West Coast. Israel should be wary of adopting California policies.) A split three-Justice Court ordered that both women be listed as the mother, in direct defiance of Israel's law that adoption can only be done by a husband and wife. The Court majority held that the minister had no right to question the legal documents showing both women as the mother. Apparently, Israel has lost the authority to define what constitutes a legal family on its soil whenever a foreign country recognizes some arrangement as a family.

In another case, the minister of education, relying on a panel of experts, determined that a program in which four teenage homosexuals discussed their sexual preferences should be made more balanced before being shown on Educational TV. A three-judge panel of the Supreme Court, including President Barak, assumed that a positive portrayal of homosexuality could have no impact on its incidence and ordered the program broadcast. Not a single statute or precedent was cited. In his comment of the case, Jonathan Rosenblum asked that we imagine a program in which four Haredi teenagers discuss their lives. If Educational TV refused to broadcast the show, "Does anyone dream that the Supreme Court would...order the program shown? The [petitioners] would more likely be assessed court costs for filing a frivolous suit." It is quite true that, in the Court's view, homosexuals are a favored class and Orthodox believers a disfavored one.

Religion

The Court's obsession with equality determined its decision in *Hoffman* v. *Director-General of the Prime Minister's Office* (2000). Overturning a practice that had existed for centuries, the Court ruled that Women of the Wall, a women's prayer group, had the right to hold prayer services at Jerusalem's Western Wall. David Hazony commented that "it has been an important judicial tradition in Israel to rule consistently for the preservation of extant practices in the holy places of all faiths" because such places are "a tinder box of sensibilities and passions." The alteration of such practices in Jewish, Christian, or Muslim shrines "risks disrupting the delicate balance which prevails in Israel among competing religious interests and between those interests and the state." Hazony said that, whatever the merits of the particular dispute, as a precedent "the ruling is potentially catastrophic."

What may save the ruling from being catastrophic is that the Court seems unlikely to extend a decision that is partly responsive to feminists among other groups. A more worrisome explanation of the decision is probably also correct. The Court has repeatedly upheld the government's prohibition of Jewish and Christian worship on the Temple Mount because such prayer would offend

Muslim sensibilities and would be liable to provoke Muslim riots. The government's argument in *Hoffman* was that women's prayer at the Western Wall would offend ultra-Orthodox sensibilities and would be liable to provoke ultra-Orthodox riots. Concern for Muslim sensibilities was reasonable, but concern for ultra-Orthodox sensibilities was not.

The Court's rejection of specifically Jewish values was also evident in its decisions that the importation of non-kosher meat may not be banned; new communities sited for defensive purposes may not be limited to Jews; and Haredi youth groups may not be funded by the government as other youth groups are. As Rosenblum wrote: "For Israeli civil libertarians, freedom from religion and the religious seems to be the highest civil liberty."

"The World Is Filled with Law"
In *Jane Doe* v. *State of Israel* (2000), three Justices sitting as the final appellate court ruled that it is criminal for a parent to use the mildest corporal punishment (e.g., a light slap on the hand) in disciplining a child. The Court did so by interpreting a provision of the Criminal Code prohibiting assault in clear violation of the Knesset's intent. The opinion purported to rely on what Gordon says "is fast becoming the Supreme Court's all-purpose justification for judicial lawmaking, the 1992 Basic Law: Human Dignity and Freedom." That *Law* says nothing, and was not intended to say anything, about reasonable spanking. Nor is the Court's

position supported by any of the other sources it cites. Worse, there was no reason for the Court to have taken up the subject. The facts of the particular case showed that a mother had clearly committed assaults on her children with violent beatings. The Court should have stopped there. Instead, it went on to legislate against mild physical discipline, an issue not before it. Not only did the Court deform the Criminal Code, but, since light and reasonable physical discipline of a child is not a violation of the civil law, the Court managed the feat of declaring that behavior that is not even a tort is a crime, punishable by two years in prison.

This, Gordon wrote, is the Court's "most significant incursion to date into Israelis' private lives." Indeed, that incursion follows from Barak's view that "the autonomy of the individual... exists because it is recognized by the law." Barak worries that some aspect of life, somewhere, may escape the Court's domination: "The moment that a certain realm is not justiciable, the wielder of power does whatever he wants." He cites the executive branch, the police, and actions taken within "normal family relations." In a word, no freedom of the individual may exist without the Court's approval.

It is possible to lament the decision as a violation of parents' personal autonomy, but it is also reasonable to view it as a radical expansion of the child's autonomy. (An increase in one person's autonomy often necessarily requires the diminishment of another's.) Much of the opinion reads that way:

> Punishment that causes pain and humiliation does
> not contribute to the child's character or educa-
> tion; it infringes on his rights as a human being. It
> damages his body, his feelings, his dignity and his
> proper development.... We must not endanger the
> physical and emotional integrity of a minor by
> administering any corporal punishment at all.

That passage reflects not merely the Court's desire to
confer radical personal autonomy on the child, but the
strain of softness and aversion to discomfort that is characteristic of modern liberalism.

Speech and Expression

The government's Film Censorship Board, which is
charged with the duty of judging a film's debauchery
according to contemporary community standards,
decided that a film was pornographic and could not be
shown. The Supreme Court, despite the judgment of a
majority of both the censorship board and the panel of
independent experts consulted, decided that the testimony of those few experts who thought the movie was
"art" was enough to warrant the film's protection on
free-speech grounds. The decision of a government body
acting responsibly and fully within its legal mandate was
overturned in favor of a free-speech principle that had no
legislative basis whatever.

Trivia

The direction of the Court's activism is indicated in cases of less gravity than those discussed above. In *Akiva Nof* v. *Ministry of Defense* the Court ruled in favor of a secular bearded man who demanded that the government supply him free of charge with a special gas mask which, unlike the ordinary masks given out to the public, could fit over a beard. The government wanted him to pay a fee, since the special mask cost the state two and a half times as much as the ordinary mask. Orthodox Jews were given the special masks free; only the secular bearded were required to pay. That distinction was correctly ruled discriminatory, and the Court could have told the government either to fund everyone or no one. Instead, the government was told to fund everyone, but the Court apparently could not resist producing a parody of New Class values. It ruled that "a beard is part of the man's self-image" and the right to determine one's self-image is implicitly protected by the *Basic Law: Human Dignity and Liberty*. Concern for radical personal autonomy, free of cost, can hardly get sillier. The Court said that there was no need to ascribe this right to any explicitly mentioned right in the law because "human dignity, as a protected constitutional value, has a broader meaning than the sum total of the recognized specific rights." That argument closely resembles the reasoning, discussed in chapter 1, by which Justice Brennan of the United States Supreme Court concluded that what the Constitution really protects is dignity, and he would decide what dignity demands, and by which Justice Douglas of the same

Court found a right of privacy broader than the sum total of recognized specific rights, although the right of privacy was not one of them.

Jewish and Democratic Values

Barak and his Court are redefining Israel's values so that, in area after area of Israeli life, the Jewishness of the state comes to matter less and less. Barak has written that Jewish values should be interpreted at the highest level of abstraction – freedom, equality, justice – so that Jewish values become indistinguishable from democratic values. In this situation, Jewish particularism disappears into the mists of abstract universalism – part of what I have called the socialist impulse – with predictably dire consequences. An Israeli court that rules on the basis of the same set of ideas as its American, Canadian, or German peers, and that insists on universalist principles, cannot sustain the particularist Jewish laws and framework set up by Israel's Zionist founders. Nor need it take account of Israel's very different and precarious situation in the Middle East. Given the centrality of the Supreme Court in Israel, the idea that Israel's Jewish character ought not to influence its decision-making is likely to influence other branches of government as well as a growing segment of the citizenry.

It is impossible not to recognize the Court's performance as one strand of a much wider weave: post-Zionism. This is a new frame of mind, propagated mainly by Israeli academics and others of the intelligentsia, that denigrates the ideals and the narrative of the Zionists who founded the Jewish nation. It is to be found in education curricula at all levels. As Yoram Hazony wrote, "The only Israeli institution likely to rival the Education Ministry in its ability to shape the Jewish character of the state of Israel is the country's Supreme Court." Education and law are each powerful forces. In tandem, they may prove overwhelming.

According to Barak, when the values of Israel as a Jewish state cannot be reconciled with its values as a democratic state, the decision must be made according to "the views of the enlightened community in Israel." The Court decides who is "enlightened" and who is not. The "enlightened community" is another term for the New Class. As Hillel Neuer points out, however, Barak's enlightened community is not a community at all; the phrase is a metaphor for a particular set of values, which is to be made dominant by judicial decision. The enlightened community holds tight to the values of universalism and progressivism, which include the defense of individual rights and equality. Given the value of universalism, in cases where the general public would prefer a value specific to Judaism, that public is effectively left without a voice or the ability to govern. A liberal world view is, willy-nilly, forced upon it.

This is very much the same, though far more explicitly expressed, as the powerful tendency of the United States Supreme Court to be influenced by the values of the academy and the intelligentsia. Barak's critics say the enlightened are an identifiable set of people recognizable by postal zip code, social affiliation, and party loyalty. In the United States a similar set is identifiable by faculty status, particularly in places such as Cambridge, New Haven, Ann Arbor, and Palo Alto; by occupation, especially journalists, professors and teachers, and television and motion picture personnel; and by politics, such as by loyalty to the Democratic Party. This "enlightened" minority has a major influence on U.S. courts, although no U.S. judge has been as imprudent as Barak in articulating that fact.

Post-Zionism appears to be the Israeli version of the counterculture prevailing among the elites of other Western nations. That counterculture, which is no longer counter but dominant, represents the outlook of the New Class. In Israel, as in the U.S., Canada, and Europe, a culture war is raging and, as in those countries, the courts take the side of the New Class minority against the general public. Judicial activism and the culture war go hand in hand, and the enlistment of the courts on one side of the war gives the New Class an extraordinarily powerful weapon. "At the end of the day," according to Neuer, "one is left with a sense that a judge who searches for the values of the 'enlightened community' is likely to find them inside himself – and then use the metaphor to justify his subjective conclusions." I once wrote of the U.S. Supreme Court that a judge who looks outside the actual Constitution looks inside himself and nowhere else. Some commentators, usually of the liberal variety, try to make the difference in judicial approaches a question of interpretation, but it is not that at all. A judge who is not bound to the original understanding of a document's principles interprets nothing but his own state of mind.

Though the displacement of democratic government by judicial rule is far advanced in many Western countries, realization of the degree to which the public has been disfranchised and the executive branch emasculated in Israel comes as a shock to most outside observers. In all probability, the more friendly to Israel such observers are, the greater the dismay. The diminution of democratic governance is worrisome enough, but an equal peril may be presented by the Supreme Court's promulgation of the abstract universalisms of equality, radical individualism, and rationalism. That this set of universalistic notions should have invaded the Israeli intelligentsia is a major threat; that it should have captured a breathtakingly imperialistic Supreme Court is a calamity. More than Israeli democracy is endangered by the New Class's post-Zionism; so, ultimately, may be Israel's survival.

Perhaps the most significant immediate outcome is that, in the face of potential Supreme Court review, the Knesset is loath to pass laws that, in its judgment, a Barak-led Court would likely overturn. In effect, Barak's "constitutional revolution" has effected a far-reaching judicial preemption, the consequences of which differ little from those of actual judicial review. To understand what might be in store for Israel once the Supreme Court actually engages in judicial review, Neuer finds it instructive to look at the experience of Canada, since it underwent a similar constitutional transformation in 1982 with the adoption of the *Charter of Rights and Freedoms*. The comparison is especially relevant because the *Charter* served Israel as a model for some of the key provisions in the

Basic Laws. This replication accounts for the strong Israeli interest in Canadian judicial and academic interpretations of the *Charter.* Several Israeli judges, Barak first among them, increasingly refer to Canadian constitutional jurisprudence.

Given its addiction to universal values, moreover, the decisions emerging from the Israel Supreme Court will likely continue to neutralize the Jewish aspect of the *Basic Law,* while causing ever-greater alienation of those "unenlightened" segments of the population who hold such values dear. The more such cases are adjudicated by a Barak-inspired Court, the less Jewish Israel is likely to become and the harder it will be to distinguish it from secular democracies such as Canada and the United States.

The Israeli public participated not at all in the alleged framing of a constitution. That public, however, has been surprisingly quiescent in the face of what could easily be described as a judicial *coup d'état.* The reasons for that passivity are probably several: the public's failure fully to comprehend what has happened; the influence of elite groups favoring judicial policy-making; a feeling that the Knesset is so politically riven as to be ineffective; and the cult of the robe: the Court's reputation as a nonpolitical body deciding fundamental matters on principle rather than from expediency or personal predilection.

The "enlightened segment" of the Israeli population does not take kindly to criticism of the role that the Barak-led Court has assigned itself. When editorials highly critical of the Court and its president appeared, the result was a torrent of denunciations − of the newspapers. Complaints were filed with the police, charging the papers and their editors with sedition and defamation. There were calls for closure of these newspapers, while prominent politicians from almost every party vied to produce the most vicious castigation of the "crime." When the chairman of the Israeli Bar Association censured the Court for intruding in matters that were properly for the Knesset, there were further denunciations, complaints to the police, and demands that the man be removed from his position both at the association and on the committee that appoints judges. The bar's ethics committee recommended that he face disciplinary charges.

After the road-closing decision, the Haredi newspapers waged a campaign against Barak, pointing out that the rule of the people had ended and that the Court was dictating on matters the Knesset should govern. Instead of finding a sympathetic audience, the entire political establishment went into outrage. Once more there were demands for indictments and drastic legal action against anybody who criticized the Court severely. That reaction came from politicians, the mainstream press, and the legal establishment.

The Haredi papers referred to Barak as the driving force behind the sophisticated battle waged against the Jewish viewpoint in Israel. He should be portrayed, the paper said, as a danger to the character of Israeli democracy and as a threat to citizens' power to decide for themselves how their country should be run. Once more, a protest against any criticism of the Court erupted and a

former Supreme Court Justice said that he was scandal-
ized that anybody had "dared to speak harshly against the
Supreme Court." There were calls for a police investigation of the papers for engaging in sedition. One chairman of a Knesset committee demanded that the
government shut down the newspapers.

Many of these attacks came from the left, but the right
also assailed critics of the Court. The legal community,
including the deans of the country's four major law
schools, issued a statement that the editorials were
intended to intimidate judges. The Association of
Municipal Attorneys asked that action be taken by the
attorney general against the papers. It was even said that
the attacks would undermine the faith of the public in
the judiciary as a whole and in the Supreme Court in
particular. An independent judiciary, it was argued, was
fundamental to the existence of the rule of law and the
preservation of a democratic regime in Israel. That was
particularly odd because there is no rule of law when
judges' personal sentiments rule and when the Court, far
from preserving the democratic regime, is undercutting
it. The Haredi papers kept up the attacks, but there were
virtually no voices defending what they had written or
the right of the papers to publish criticism. The attorney
general declined to act on any of the criminal complaints
because, to do so, would infringe on the freedom of
speech and cause more harm than benefit, but he still
made it clear that he did not oppose social pressure to
suppress the writers' views. He said that one of the disad-
vantages of an indictment was that a publicized trial

would give the editorialists another platform from which to express their views. Even Prime Minister Netanyahu decried what he called unrestrained attacks on the Court and its Justices. The American Bar Association's attacks on critics of activist American courts pales by comparison with the fury unleashed in Israel.

Israel has set a standard for judicial imperialism that can probably never be surpassed, and, one devoutly hopes, will never be equaled elsewhere. The sad irony is that the Supreme Court, operating with a *Basic Law* that specifies the values to be applied as those of Israel as both a Jewish and democratic state, is gradually producing an Israel that is neither Jewish nor democratic.

4

THE INTERNATIONALIZATION OF LAW

In less than a decade, an unprecedented concept has emerged to submit international politics to judicial procedures. It has spread with extraordinary speed and has not been subject to systematic debate, partly because of the intimidating passion of its advocates . . . . The danger is that it is being pushed to extremes which risk substituting the tyranny of judges for that of governments; historically the dictatorship of the virtuous has often led to inquisitions and even witch hunts.

Henry Kissinger

The internationalization of law is happening with phenomenal speed and comprehensiveness. With that development comes law's seemingly inevitable accompaniment: judicial activism. For some, usually those on the left, internationalism appears to be almost unalloyed good. The use of armed force between nations, it is said, must be tamed by being brought within a rule of law. The violation of human rights by nations against their own citizens must be diminished or ended by holding the perpetrators responsible in international tribunals or, in some cases, in other national court systems that are willing to take jurisdiction. International codes of individual freedom, similar in intention to the United States' *Bill of Rights*, are enacted to protect persons from majoritarian rule.

To many people these goals seem entirely laudable, and so they would be if the realities lived up to the abstractions. But that outcome is impossible. Instead, internationalization will magnify many times over the defects already identified in the constitutional law of the United States, Canada, and Israel: the loss of democratic government, the incursion of politics into law, and the coerced movement of the culture to the left. The New Class is an international class and it displays its socialist impulse everywhere while waging an international culture war. The internationalization of law is one way of transforming parallel struggles in the various nations of the West into a single struggle waged across national boundaries. The explanation for this internationalization of law may contain an even more sinister element. The New Class in the United States has failed to press its full liberal agenda in Congress, the state legislatures, and, to some extent, in federal and state courts. By creating international law, a project at which it is particularly adept, the New Class hopes not only to outflank American legislatures and courts but to have liberal views adopted at a different level and then imposed on the United States. History shows that the citizens of individual nations have been unable and unwilling to resist the depredations of their national courts. There is no reason to expect they will be able to resist courts that are sitting in foreign countries, composed of judges of several nationalities, and operating under vague humanistic standards to which their own nations have, however ambiguously, pledged allegiance.

It will be possible to discuss only a few examples of judicial activism in the international arena. Conventions and treaties exist on most subjects: human rights; civil and political rights; economic, social, and cultural rights; genocide; racial discrimination; and discrimination against women. In addition to the committees and councils that supervise aspects of these prohibitions and guarantees, several courts have jurisdiction in different areas: the International Court of Justice (World Court); the European Court of Human Rights; the European Court of Justice; and the not-yet-operative International Criminal Court. Given the limitations of a single chapter, the discussion here will center on human rights and the use of armed force between nations.

The internationalization of law and the corresponding internationalization of judicial activism take various forms. The first is the recent tendency of national courts, when applying their own constitutions, to cite the decisions of foreign courts in applying their own constitutions. An allied form is international conferences of judges, professors, and social activists to discuss the means of creating new rights in each nation. One primary example was a conference held in London in 1999 to consider ways of making homosexual conduct a constitutional right in various nations.

Some national courts have agreed to try cases involving acts done abroad by foreign nationals against foreign nationals. Thus, some United States courts have accepted the jurisdiction to hear tort claims for actions that have no connection with the United States or its citizens. Other nations' courts have claimed the authority to apply criminal sanctions to conduct having no relation to their own countries. The most prominent international tribunal in this area is the European Court of Human Rights sitting in Strasbourg.

What is called "customary international law" is used to pronounce judgment on the use of armed force by nations, despite the fact that there is no international law established by custom. If there were, it would not restrain international aggression but unleash it. The Nuremberg trials in the wake of World War II confirmed both the notion of such law and the idea that it represented civilized behavior. Those trials served two valuable purposes: they created a detailed history of the horrors perpetrated by the Third Reich, and they provided moral justification for the imprisonment or execution of those responsible. They should have been left at that, but the winning powers felt a need to justify the proceedings further by claiming that, before the Nazi regime came to power, an international law existed which forbade wars of aggression and the deliberate murder by a nation of its own citizens. No law justified the punishments meted out, though there was a moral necessity for them. The victors lacked the stomach to say that, however. Soon we became addicted to the idea of international law and began the proliferation of what we chose to call "laws" that guaranteed every good thing.

In recent years there has been a proliferation of international tribunals that apply treaties or codes of some kind to all nations that have succumbed to internal pressure to sign on to them. Some of these courts claim jurisdiction only over European nations, but others claim a global jurisdiction that they are powerless to enforce.

Many of the judgments of international courts are unenforceable, in the sense that the judgment of an Illinois state court, for example, is enforceable anywhere in the United States. The judgment of the Illinois court is made effective, if necessary, by force. International tribunals can summon no such assistance and, as a result, such judgments are widely ignored. But that does not make the judgments harmless. In the first place, some of these judgments are enforceable and great injustices may be done to individuals caught in their highly politicized toils. More than that, the proceedings in some international tribunals take on the aspect of show trials and their judgments often carry great moral weight. It is here that these courts become not merely allies of the New Class in the culture war but allies of the left in the international war of political propaganda. The United States is particularly unlikely to win in such forums.

International law is not law but politics. For that reason, it is dangerous to give the name law, which summons up respect, to political struggles that are essentially lawless. The problem is not merely the anti-Americanism that grips foreign elites and shapes law; it is also the American intellectual class, which is largely hostile to America and uses international law, or what is claimed to be international law, to attack the morality of its own government and society. International law becomes one more weapon in the domestic culture war. It must be admitted, moreover, that the United States has used its power to force the trials of some men who have done no worse than other men with whom we do not interfere, whether from hesitation to pay the costs in casualties or from calculations of national economic advantage. That may or may not be justifiable, but it hardly bespeaks devotion to law.

Human Rights

The insidious appeal of internationalism is illustrated by the fact that some Justices of the American Supreme Court have begun to look to foreign decisions and even to foreign legislation for guidance in interpreting the American Constitution. Perhaps it is significant that the Justices who do so are from the liberal wing of the Court. This trend is not surprising, given liberalism's tendency to search for the universal and to denigrate the particular.

In *Thompson* v. *Oklahoma* (1988) Justice Stevens, writing for four members of an equally divided Court, held that, for a state to execute a person who had committed a crime when he was fifteen years of age, the punishment was cruel, unusual, and unconstitutional. In the course of his argument, Stevens said that conclusion was "consistent with the views that have been expressed by respected professional organizations, by other nations that share our Anglo-American heritage, and by the leading members of the Western European community." He continued: "We have previously recognized the relevance of the views of the international community in determining whether a punishment is cruel and unusual." That relevance, nevertheless, remains unclear. Mixed in with foreign materials concerning the execution of juveniles was a list of nations that had abolished the death penalty altogether, again by legislation rather than judicial decree. The Justice also cited three human rights treaties, two of which had been signed but not ratified by the United States; the third treaty was the Geneva Convention concerning the protection of civilians in time of war.

The dissent of Justice Brennan was similar in *Stanford* v. *Kentucky* (1989), a case that allowed the imposition of capital punishment for a crime committed when the defendant was sixteen or seventeen years of age: "Together, the rejection of the death penalty for juveniles by a majority of the States, the rarity of the sentence for juveniles, both as an absolute and a comparative matter, the decisions of respected organizations in relevant fields that this punishment is unacceptable, and its rejection generally throughout the world, provide to my mind a strong grounding that it is not constitutionally tolerable that certain States persist in authorizing the execution of adolescent offenders."

More recently, in *Printz* v. *United States* (2000), Justice Breyer dissented from a decision that it is unconstitutional for a federal gun control statute to require state officials to carry out the federal policy. Rather, he found foreign views of federalism helpful in construing the requirements of federalism in the United States: "Of course, we are interpreting our own Constitution, not those of other nations, and there may be relevant political and structural differences between their system and our own....But their experience may nonetheless cast an empirical light on the consequences of different solutions to a common legal problem – in this case the problem of reconciling central authority with the need to preserve the liberty enhancing autonomy of a smaller constituent governmental entity." He thought the experience of European countries confirmed the answer that was implied in the question Justice Stevens had asked: "Why, or how, would what the majority sees as a constitutional alternative – the creation of a new federal gun law bureaucracy, or the expansion of an existing federal bureaucracy – better promote either state sovereignty or individual liberty?"

Justice Breyer looked abroad for constitutional guidance in two other cases. He concurred in *Nixon* v. *Missouri* (2000), a case that upheld a state's campaign finance limitations against a free speech challenge. He found the approach taken in some federal cases "consistent with that

of other constitutional courts facing similar complex constitutional problems," and he cited decisions of the
European Court of Human Rights and a Canadian court.
But in *Knight* v. *Florida* (1999) this tendency to look
abroad for guidance to the meaning of the American
Constitution became risible. Breyer stated that he found
"useful" decisions concerning allowable delays of execution by the Privy Council of Jamaica, the Supreme Court
of India, and the Supreme Court of Zimbabwe.

The question in each of these cases should have been
the understanding of the ratifiers of the *Bill of Rights* in
1791, not the current views of foreign nations. In any
event, these views were often expressed in legislation
rather than in judicial decisions. If the views of foreign
legislatures are relevant, they would surely be relevant to
debates in American legislatures, not to judicial interpretations of the American Constitution. Nor is it clear
what relevance the list of nations that have abolished the
death penalty has to the United States Constitution,
which repeatedly assumes in explicit language that the
death penalty is available to federal and state governments
should they care to use it. If we disregard such noncon-
stitutional considerations as the policies of most states, the
rarity of the punishment, or the views of respected
organizations, it is remarkable that "the standards of
decency in the form of legislation in other countries" are
thought to have any bearing at all on the historical meaning of the American Constitution. Finally, with regard to
federalism, Breyer was right – if the Court's function is
legislative. It then makes sense to look to foreign

concepts of federalism for guidance. It does not make sense, however, if the Court is applying the concept of federalism embodied in the American design as it is expressed in the Constitution.

There are other examples of Justices citing foreign decisions, both judicial and legislative, as relevant to their interpretation of the American Constitution. Nor is this phenomenon exclusively American. The Supreme Courts of Canada and of Israel, the other two national judiciaries discussed in this book, have done the same thing and have also relied on international conventions, United Nations resolutions, and other materials. The inevitable result of all these practices is the international homogenization of constitutional law. It can be accomplished only if the various national courts are willing to minimize the historical understanding of their own constitutions in favor of what they perceive as an international morality.

The fever for internationalizing law through national judiciaries surfaced at the American Bar Association's annual meeting in 2000 held in London. Four American Supreme Court Justices were present, but Anthony Kennedy bore the brunt of the attack on the Court's alleged "insularity." A prominent London barrister rose to accuse the United States Supreme Court of "turning its back on the Continent," noting that the Justices rarely cite the decisions of European courts: "Your system is quite certain it has nothing much to learn from us." Some Americans rose to promise that our courts would do better in future. The dean of a major law school said that several Justices had been active in moving the Court to a more internationalist approach, which "has begun to permeate the entire system." The mayor of Detroit was even more defensive: "We're not as parochial as one might think." While British courts might be in the forefront now in citing European decisions, he promised American lawyers and judges will eventually take the lead so that, "at the end of the day, we will be ahead."

Kennedy, to his credit, did not succumb to this combination of insolent foreign browbeating and pusillanimous American response. If American courts cede authority to remote courts unknown to the public, he said, there was a risk of losing the allegiance of the people. American courts, moreover, are often unsure whether European courts are referring to the same issues that the Justices must decide. Contrary to Breyer's position, Kennedy stated that European federalism "has nothing to do with our federalism." He was quite right. European courts deal with different constitutions, cultures, histories, and political systems from those the American Court must consider.

Another American route to internationalization has been created by the resurrection of the *Alien Tort Claims Act*, a law enacted in 1789 of somewhat mysterious intention that had lain dormant for two hundred years. The statute provides: "The district courts shall have original jurisdiction of any civil action by an alien for tort only, committed in violation of the law of nations or a treaty of the United States." The statute owes its reinvigoration to a similar expansion in the concept of the law of nations. *Filartiga* v. *Pena-Irala* broke the silence in 1980 by awarding damages in a suit by Paraguayans residing in the United States for the murder in Paraguay of a Paraguayan by a Paraguayan official. No such jurisdiction was contemplated in 1789 because the law of nations then had a much narrower scope. The court, as Professor Jeremy Rabkin put it, "cheered on by a host of international law scholars, insisted, however, that 'customary international law' has greatly expanded and now incorporates an international law of human rights." The Paraguayan official, safe in his own country, saw no reason to "pay anything to anybody on the mere say-so of a U.S. court." That is the common fate of such judgments. These suits do not really seek recompense, but aspire only to make a propaganda point more morally compelling by the decision of a U.S. court.

In 1984 the appeals court on which I sat heard a similar case, *Tel-Oren* v. *Libyan Arab Republic*. The case grew out of an armed attack on a civilian bus in Israel in which sixty-five people were seriously injured and twenty-nine killed. Survivors and representatives of those killed sued Libya, the Palestine Liberation Organization, and others. Though unanimous in rejecting the claim put forward, the three judges did not agree on the rationale. My reason for denying that the plaintiffs had a cause of action was that the claim defendants "violated customary principles of international law against terrorism...an area of international law in which there is little or no consensus and in which the disagreements concern politically sensitive issues that are especially prominent in the foreign relations problems of the Middle East." The lack of clarity in the legal principles involved, the absence of consensus about those principles, and the impingement of the case on America's foreign relations all led to the conclusion that the case was not appropriate for federal court adjudication.

A major problem with the modern application of the *Alien Tort Claims Act* is, as one judge expressed it, that "[t]his old but little used section is a kind of legal Lohengrin...no one seems to know whence it came." Along the same line, I wrote that "[h]istorical research has not yet disclosed what [the Act] was intended to accomplish. That fact poses a special problem for courts. A statute whose original meaning is hidden from us and yet which, if its words are read incautiously, with modern assumptions in mind, is capable of plunging our nation into foreign conflicts, ought to be approached by the judiciary with great circumspection. It will not do simply to assert that the statutory phrase, the 'law of nations,' whatever it may have meant in 1789, must be read today as incorporating all the modern rules of international law.... It is important to remember that in 1789 there was no concept of international human rights; neither was there, under the traditional version of customary international law, any recognition of a right of private parties to recover."

Blackstone, who was thoroughly familiar to Americans when the Constitution and the statute were written, said that the principal offenses against the law of nations were violation of safe conduct, infringement of the rights of ambassadors, and piracy. American adoption of that law in the *Alien Tort Claims Act* was probably intended, by providing a remedy, to avoid giving offense to powerful foreign nations. That would explain the law against violations of safe conduct and infringement of the rights of ambassadors. (Piracy was a violation of the law of nations because no single nation had jurisdiction over acts done on the high seas.) The modern expansion of the concept of the law of nations, in which American courts augment tensions with foreign nations, is quite the opposite of what was intended. It is preposterous to think that a small, weak nation clinging to the Atlantic coast took upon itself the task of judging torts by foreigners against foreigners in foreign nations such as Great Britain and France. "[I]t will not do," I wrote, "to insist that the judge's duty is to construe the statute in order not to flout the will of Congress. On these topics, we have, at the moment, no evidence what the intention of Congress was. When courts lack such evidence, to 'construe' is to legislate, to act in the dark, and hence to do many things that, it is virtually certain, Congress did not intend."

My view has not prevailed; *Filartiga*'s approach has become the norm. American courts are freely judging tort claims that have not the remotest connection to the United States. Five Chinese natives sued the former Chinese prime minister, Li Peng, for his role in the Tiananmen Square crackdown that killed hundreds of civilians in Beijing. President Robert Mugabe of Zimbabwe was served with a civil suit for $400 million while he was visiting the United States because he had allegedly ordered killings and torture in his country. President Slobodan Milosevic of the former Yugoslavia was sued here, as were the Prince of Wales and Prime Minister Margaret Thatcher, on the claim that they had violated human rights in both Northern Ireland and Libya. The Prince and Thatcher were held to have immunity. A federal court jury awarded $4.5 billion in damages against Radovan Karadzic, the Bosnian Serb leader, to people who were raped, tortured, or the survivors of those killed in the Balkan conflict.

The modern expansion of the *Alien Tort Claims Act* is judicial activism – indeed, moral presumption – at its highest pitch. The law of nations incorporated into American tort law in 1789 bears almost no resemblance to the law of nations being applied by U.S. courts today.

Some national courts have begun to assert universal criminal jurisdiction – the authority to try persons for acts in other countries. Thus, a Belgian court, having been given such jurisdiction by the legislature, tried and convicted Rwandan nuns for actions during a massacre in Rwanda. The case that attracted the most attention, however, involved the former head of Chile's government, General Augusto Pinochet. While Pinochet was recovering from surgery in London, a Spanish judge issued an international warrant for his arrest. The judge claimed authority to prosecute Pinochet under international law as well as Spain's domestic law. Jurisdiction was claimed despite objections by Chile, which had worked out its own settlement with Pinochet. A British judge then issued a provisional warrant for extradition, and Pinochet was arrested in the hospital. The House of Lords relied on international conventions said to be incorporated into the criminal statutes of the United Kingdom and held that Pinochet lacked immunity because acts of torture could not be regarded as functions of a head of state. The home secretary, after initially authorizing extradition proceedings, ultimately allowed Pinochet to return to Chile as not medically fit to stand trial.

David Rivkin and Lee Casey note that the modern notion of universal jurisdiction would "permit the courts of any state to prosecute and punish the leadership of any other state for violations of international humanitarian norms":

> [T]he rule's proponents should keep in mind that any independent state, not just "right thinking" Western ones, would be entitled to prosecute such "violations" on a universal jurisdiction approach. Most recently, the courts of Yugoslavia tried (*in absentia*) and convicted the NATO leaders responsible for the spring 1999 air campaign against Serbia for crimes against humanity. (President Clinton was sentenced to twenty years imprisonment.) This proceeding was obviously absurd. Yet legally, it was just as "legitimate" as Spain's attempt to prosecute Pinochet.

It is somewhat nauseating to hear of law forbidding "crimes against humanity" when it is obvious that what is involved is not law but politicized force. Both French and Spanish courts, it's worth noting, have dismissed Pinochet-type proceedings against Fidel Castro. This "law" applies only to leaders and citizens of small, powerless countries on the right, while the most murderous leaders of powerful or leftist countries (China and Cuba, for instance) are courted, flattered, and fêted. Moral law, stable law, cannot be made out of sheer hypocrisy, but that is what the arrest and proposed extradition of Pinochet amounted to. International law in such matters is little more than organized hypocrisy.

The difference that power makes is illustrated by the contrast between Pinochet's vulnerability and Clinton's invulnerability and the fate of Milosevic. He was deported from Yugoslavia to The Hague to be tried before the International Criminal Tribunal. The Serbian legislature refused to extradite him, intending that he be tried in Yugoslavia. The Serbian government ordered him extradited by decree, but, when the constitutional court put the decree on hold, the Serbian government ignored the court. Far from being a testament to international law, Charles Krauthammer explained, what was demonstrated was American economic power. Milosevic was arrested on April 1, 2001, because the U.S. Congress set that deadline. If it was not met, the United States would withhold $50 million in reconstruction aid. Then "Milosevic was spirited out of the country. Why precisely on June 28? Because on the very next day, a donors' conference of Western nations would be meeting to consider the Serbs' request for $1.25 billion in reconstruction aid. They knew they wouldn't get it – the U.S. was not even prepared to send a delegation – until it was clear that Milosevic would be deported. Money talks." Though Krauthammer, along with most of us, wants Milosevic to pay for his crimes, his punishment will not vindicate international law. Other men with blood on their hands walk free. All that was proved is that the United States, like other nations, can and will manipulate governments and call the manipulation dedication to international justice.

The implications of these episodes, particularly Pinochet's, are not yet entirely clear, but, at a minimum, it is safe to say that former and current government officials have to pay attention to their travel plans. The degree of danger officials face will depend on the power and influence of their countries. The Chilean judge who indicted Pinochet when he returned home prepared a list of questions for Henry Kissinger concerning his knowledge about the death of an American shortly after Pinochet took power. The Chilean Supreme Court approved and the questions were forwarded to the U.S. State Department. Kissinger will not dignify the proceedings by answering the questions.

No such assurance can be felt by officials of less powerful nations. Israel's Foreign Ministry, for example, has warned its government, army, and security officials to be cautious about traveling to certain countries. Some might level charges concerning the violation of Palestinians' human rights. Among the nations that may claim universal jurisdiction to try Israelis are Belgium, Britain, and Spain. Probably there are others. There is an attempt in Belgium to indict Ariel Sharon, Israel's prime minister, on the ground that he should have stopped a massacre in Lebanon by Christian militiamen allied with Israel. Israelis, according to the *New York Times*, "see the Belgian case as an example of European pro-Arab, anti-Israel and perhaps even anti-Jewish bias." They are probably right. Violations of human rights in Arab countries, Israelis say, are far worse than anything Israel can be charged with. There do not appear, however, to be any attempts to charge Arab officials or the Palestine Liberation Organization with any crimes.

Issues of international human rights do not, of course, depend entirely on the assumption by national courts of universal jurisdiction. Of equal interest and greater importance is the *European Convention for Protection of Human Rights and Fundamental Freedoms*. Both the Convention and the new concept of universal jurisdiction just discussed are transforming international law from a body of rules, however ill-founded, ambiguous, and ineffective, about the conduct of nations in relation to one another into a body of rules about the rights of individuals against their own nations.

The Convention's rules are interpreted by the European Court of Human Rights at Strasbourg. The Court's decisions are binding on those nations that have agreed to its jurisdiction. The Convention contains the right to life, the prohibition of torture, the right to liberty and security, the right to respect for private and family life, the freedom of expression, and the prohibition of discrimination. Amendments or protocols contain additional rights and prohibitions, but not all have been ratified by all the states. Some states, such as Germany and Great Britain, have incorporated the Convention and the Strasbourg court's interpretations of it into their domestic laws. The courts of these countries will themselves apply the Convention without requiring litigants to appeal to Strasbourg to obtain a ruling. Both before and after incorporation, the Convention, as interpreted by activist judges, has had a marked effect on British autonomy and culture. Significantly, the Labour government made incorporation a major part of its program, while conservatives opposed the move. That reaction is typical of developments everywhere. The left wants expanded judicial review in the name of rights because it has seen what has happened in the United States and other nations which have taken that course. Conservatives oppose the move for the same reason. English judging will soon be politicized, as will the selection of English judges. Britain signed the European Convention in 1953, but did not make it part of domestic law for nearly fifty years.

With the incorporation of the Convention into English domestic law, a flood of cases about rights is certain to occur, and many more English laws will be declared invalid. A judge has thrown out a case against two men charged with speeding on the ground that requiring them to say which of them was driving violated their right against self-incrimination. Once the rhetoric of rights takes hold, the law is applied reflexively, according to semantics and without regard to the reason that defines and limits the right. The coerced movement to the cultural left is predictable and familiar. The Labour government knew what it was doing. Those enchanted by the idea of the protection of basic rights did not understand. The dream is on the side of the left; the unchangeable reality is on the right.

In *Dudgeon* v. *United Kingdom* (1981) the European
Court of Human Rights ruled that, under the article
guaranteeing respect for family life, Northern Ireland's
anti-sodomy laws were invalid. Despite the deference
("margin of appreciation") due to government authorities in the protection of morals, less deference was due
here because the subject "concerns the most intimate
aspects of private life." The Court "cannot overlook the
marked changes which have occurred in this regard in
the domestic law of member states." There was, of
course, no reason to require Northern Ireland to conform its policy on morals to that of other nations except
that the Court, like many courts in the Western world,
disapproves of judgments that homosexual behavior
is immoral.

Smith and Grady v. *United Kingdom* (1999) held that
two members of the Royal Air Force could not be dismissed for homosexuality. A recent study by the Ministry
of Defence upholding the policy of barring homosexuals from the armed forces was found not convincing
because it was based on "negative attitudes." The Court
noted that European countries with similar policies were
now in a small minority. Once more, the Court said it
could not overlook "the widespread and consistently
developing views and associated legal changes in the
domestic laws of Contracting States on this issue." British
deference to government decisions – expressed in the
"irrationality" doctrine – insufficiently protected the
individual's right to privacy because it did not correspond
to the Court of Human Rights' tests that the ban rest on

"pressing social need" and be "proportionate to legitimate state ends." It is indicative of judicial attitudes that, in the British decisions upholding the policy, the judges had lamented the level of deference British law required them to give. *Smith and Grady* was decided on the same day as *Lustig-Prean and Beckett* v. *United Kingdom*, which ruled that homosexuals had a right to serve in the Royal Navy. That case was filed in 1996, just months after Parliament voted to uphold the ban on such service.

The United Kingdom's *Sexual Offences Act* of 1967 decriminalized private consensual homosexual conduct between adults, but made an exception to permit punishment of group sex. In *ADT* v. *United Kingdom* (2000), the police had found a videotape of the applicant engaging in sex with four other men. Yet the Court unanimously held that the applicant's conviction for gross indecency was wrongful and awarded damages and expenses. In *A.* v. *United Kingdom* (1998) the state was held responsible for not protecting a nine-year-old boy from "inhuman or degrading treatment or punishment." His stepfather, the legal guardian, had hit him with a garden cane. Though a British jury acquitted the stepfather on his defense of "reasonable chastisement," the Court held that "the law did not provide adequate protection" to secure rights and freedoms.

The court broadened its jurisdiction by making the United Kingdom responsible for potential actions in the United States. *Soering* v. *United Kingdom* (1989) involved a German national residing in the United Kingdom and suspected of a double murder in Virginia. The Court ruled that if the United Kingdom extradited Soering, that action would constitute a violation of the Convention's prohibition of torture. Physical and mental suffering while awaiting execution, it said, amounted to a "death row phenomenon" that would be degrading and inhuman treatment. To obtain Soering's extradition, Virginia had to agree not to charge him with a capital offense.

Similarly, in *Open Door and Dublin Well Woman* v. *Ireland* (1992), Ireland was held precluded, on the grounds of freedom of expression, from prohibiting the dissemination of information about overseas abortion clinics.

The certainty of abuse of international tribunals is illustrated by the lawsuit that has been filed in the European Court of Human Rights in Strasbourg by relatives of Argentine sailors who died when Britain sank the battleship *General Belgrano* on May 2, 1982, during the Falklands war. Damages are sought from the British government. The Court is asked at a considerable remove in time, distance, and knowledge to judge a combat action during war. The claimed competence of a court to judge a wartime military action is especially illegitimate because a judgment against Britain would override the agreement worked out between the two countries that the sinking was "a legal act of war."

It is not clear why most of the Human Rights Court's decisions on cultural matters appear to involve the United Kingdom. Perhaps it is due to other nations accepting the convention as domestic law, and the United Kingdom not taking that step until 2000. Thus, many cultural issues may have been settled in conformity with the court's interpretation of the convention without reaching Strasbourg. It is clear, in any event, that in cultural matters (decided under the rubric of "human rights") the Strasbourg court displays the tendencies of the New Class. The court is activist, quick to displace democratic government (despite lip service to deference or the "margin of appreciation"), and pushes the various European cultures to the left. A feature of the latter trend is a mental or psychological softness, an unwillingness to allow elected governments to make traditional moral judgments about behavior. Nonjudgmentalism becomes a virtue enforced by the court, at least when the judgments condemned accord with bourgeois values.

The presumption of international tribunals was well illustrated in the *LaGrand* case, *Germany* v. *United States of America* (1999), when the International Court of Justice (ICJ or World Court) ordered the United States to heed violations of the Vienna Convention on Consular Relations during death penalty proceedings. The LaGrand brothers had committed a murder in Arizona and a jury in that state gave them the death penalty. Though residing in the United States, the brothers were German nationals. The ICJ held, in effect, that its version of the treaty superseded both the American Constitution and state law and directed that the United States "should take all measures at its disposal to ensure that Walter LaGrand is not executed pending the final decision in these proceedings, and should inform the Court of all the measures which it has taken in implementation of this Order." When the U.S. Supreme Court rejected Germany's attempt to obtain enforcement of the ICJ's order, the execution of Walter LaGrand was carried out. The ICJ insisted that its orders were binding on American and other national courts and stated that, with respect to future convictions carrying serious penalties, "it would be incumbent on the United States to allow the review and reconsideration of the conviction and sentence by taking account of the violation of the rights set forth in the [Vienna Convention]." The ICJ had no authority to give orders to the United States and its courts. The decision was an example of the judicial activism that is rapidly becoming characteristic of international tribunals.

The next international outrage on the horizon is the proposed International Criminal Court. The treaty establishing the court will go into effect when sixty nations have ratified it. At the end of 2000, 139 nations had signed the treaty and 27 had ratified it. Despite expressing concerns about the treaty's flaws, the United States signed but has no intention of ratifying. One of those flaws is that the court would have jurisdiction over a crime when either the state where the crime was committed or the state of the perpetrator is a party to the treaty or consented to jurisdiction. This term means, for example, that if an American allegedly committed a crime in a country that had ratified the treaty, the court would claim jurisdiction to try him even though America had not accepted the treaty. Alternatively, if Yugoslavia didn't ratify and then massacred some of its own citizens, the ICC would have no jurisdiction. But if the United States, which had ratified, used armed force to stop the massacre, American personnel could be tried. That possible reprisal could deter the United States from meeting its obligations to its allies or participating in humanitarian interventions.

The court will be a powerful arm of the prosecution. The main concern is not that the prosecutor will indict a soldier who has committed a war crime, but that a political prosecutor might select particular targets: the president, cabinet officers on the National Security Council, and other senior officials responsible for defense and foreign policy. That concern should be shared by all nations that use armed force abroad, whether in the conduct of a war or of peace-keeping operations. The court has no rules of procedure, no protection for the rights of the accused comparable with those of the United States, and no clear separation between prosecutors and judges.

To make matters worse, the statutes the ICC must enforce are intolerably vague and fertile grounds for judicial activism. "War crimes," for example, include "[i]ntentionally launching an attack in the knowledge that such an attack will cause incidental loss of life or injury to civilians or damage to civilian objects or widespread, long-term and severe damage to the natural environment which would be clearly excessive in relation to the concrete and direct overall military advantage to be anticipated." Nobody can know in advance what that sentence means. Almost all attacks unavoidably cause harm to civilians and to the natural environment. How is a field commander to know what he may or may not order under a wide range of largely unforeseeable circumstances? Taken seriously, the statute would paralyze an army's capacity to fight.

Taken cynically, as it should be, the statute provides cover for politically motivated reprisals after the event, reprisals undertaken by judges in the guise of law.

Nor are the current list of ambiguously worded crimes the end of the damage that is contemplated. The representative of the International Law Commission that produced the original draft treaty said, "[L]et us think about ways in which new developments in substantive law and even new crimes can be brought within the jurisdiction of the Court as time passes and the law progresses."

Though it is not possible here to explore the subject in the detail it deserves, a word should be added about the way in which international law "progresses" and new law, especially human rights law, is created. In furtherance of their own imperialistic ambitions, courts are inclined to give weight to international statements such as the various United Nations declarations and resolutions. These statements are the product not only of governments responding to their own interests and constituencies but also of nongovernmental organizations, or NGOs, that participate in the processes by which such declarations and resolutions are made. The NGOs are typically highly ideological participants at the United Nations and in conferences under UN auspices around the world. Feminist NGOs, for example, lobby for universal rights of abortion and for mandatory proportional (50 per cent) representation in legislatures. Their influence often approximates that of governments in the formation of norms that are then said to be international law. Academics are another powerful group. Many of them maintain that their articles and their speeches at conferences constitute evidence of international law. The claims of NGOs and academics do nothing to lessen the ambiguity and opacity or to heighten the legitimacy of that law. Yet it is claimed that nations have no choice but to adhere to law made in this fashion.

Jack Goldsmith quotes an international law scholar: "States really never make international law on the subject of human rights," but rather "it is made by the people that care; the professors, the writers of textbooks and casebooks, and the authors of articles in leading international law journals." As Goldsmith says, "In a discipline that views its scholarship as a source of law, it is no surprise that this scholarship is characterized by policy prescriptions that reflect author preferences, or criticisms of practices deemed to violate international law. These tendencies are exacerbated by a powerful idealism. International law academics tend to see themselves as part of an 'invisible college' devoted to world justice." To the degree that judges take these scholars seriously, it is hardly surprising that international human rights law continually moves to the cultural left.

The Use of Armed Force

One of the great deceptions practiced by proponents of international law is that there is something deserving the name of "law" by which the use of armed force between nations may be controlled or at least inhibited to some worthwhile degree. In fact, there is no such law, and the pretense that it exists is a harmful fantasy.

It is difficult to believe that anyone supposes that the use of armed force between nations will be deterred by treaties or by customary international law. Treaties are tissue barriers to tanks and military aircraft. Customary international law is of even less value. We have, however, a long history of naivety in these matters. Sixty-two nations, including Germany, Italy, and Japan, signed the Kellogg-Briand Pact of 1928. The pact condemned "recourse to war for the solution of international controversies." Japan invaded Manchuria in 1931, Italy attacked Ethiopia in 1935, Germany occupied Austria in 1938 and began World War II by invading Poland in 1939. Hitler claimed allegiance to the pact throughout his previous aggressions in Europe. The entire enterprise of controlling armed force by "law" accomplishes little other than teaching disrespect for law and serving as the basis for accusations of lawlessness during and after the fighting.

The major difficulty with international law is that it converts what are essentially problems of international morality, as defined by a particular political community, into arguments about law that are largely drained of morality. This conversion is, no doubt, a conscious tactic of the left. When there is danger that a nation's public might support the action the left dislikes, the charge is made that it violates law. Government officials are then drawn into quibbles about nonexistent laws that inevitably divert the public from the merits of what was done to the charge that the nation in question, usually the United States, is an international outlaw.

While their social and cultural predilections are much the same, members of the international New Class are not unified on all subjects. There are themes that cut across otherwise common values. There is, for example, a widespread resentment of the United States, particularly among the intelligentsia of many foreign nations, a resentment that finds expression in international law. A similar hostility is directed at Israel by Arab and some European nations. There is also antagonism between have and have-not nations, between developed countries and those still developing or still awaiting the first signs of development. This antagonism often takes the form of demands for the redistribution of wealth and power from the nations of the North to those of the South.

The anti-Americanism that frequently suffuses international tribunals was exemplified by the decision of the International Court of Justice that the United States had violated customary international law by aiding the Nicaraguan insurgency of the contras against the Sandanista dictatorship, including the mining of Nicaraguan harbors. When the United States learned in 1984 that Nicaragua would file a claim in the ICJ, it suspended its acceptance of the tribunal's jurisdiction over disputes with any Central American nation. When the ICJ decided it would retain jurisdiction, the United States terminated its qualified 1946 acceptance of the court's compulsory jurisdiction. At the time, only 47 of the 162 nations entitled to accept that jurisdiction did so – and nine of the fifteen judges came from nations that did not.

El Salvador was under attack from armed rebels

supported by Nicaragua, but the court rejected that country's petition to intervene, although the ICJ's own statute
gave El Salvador that right. Nicaragua alone was to be
heard. The ICJ had no jurisdiction under the treaties
invoked by Nicaragua, so the court decided it could apply
customary international law whose principles were said to
be binding despite their incorporation in the treaties that
could not be applied. Its application of those principles
was particularly lawless, and the principles themselves
turned out to be one-sided, wooden, and wholly unsuited
to the realities of international armed conflict.

The court found that Nicaragua, despite supporting,
arming, and giving sanctuary to the rebels attacking El
Salvador's government, had not engaged in armed attack.
That finding, however contrary to fact and common
sense, should have ended the case. There was no reason to
go on to address the United States's claim that it was exer-
cising the well-established right of collective self-defense.
But the court chose to do so and rejected the claim for a
very odd reason: the state undergoing attack must declare
that fact. Another state may not exercise the right of collective self-defense based on its assessment of the situation.

This entirely novel requirement had a major impact.
Even if El Salvador was under attack by Nicaragua and
the entire world knew it, but El Salvador, for reasons of
prudence, did not wish to make a formal declaration to
that effect, the United States could not respond by treat-
ing Nicaragua in the same way that Nicaragua was treat-
ing El Salvador. Still worse, El Salvador had, in fact, asked
the United States to assist in its defense, President Duarte

had repeatedly mentioned the attack in press conferences, and El Salvador's improperly rejected petition to intervene in the ICJ's proceedings had declared the existence of such an attack. When the decision inevitably went against it, the United States did not, of course, pay damages, nor had Nicaragua expected it to.

The purpose and effect of the invocation of the ICJ's jurisdiction (which did not exist) was to inflict a serious political and moral injury to the United States. That was true in America as well as abroad. International law scholarship, along with the rest of the American academic world, is politicized. One of the characteristics of the American academy is the hostility to America that flourishes there. For every professor who criticized the ICJ's obviously illegitimate decision, another castigated the United States. No Nicaraguan scholar criticized the decision, which is one more example of how international law about the use of force harms only open, democratic nations and not dictatorships. As Professor Michael Reisman pointed out, the "international law-making process has itself undergone change and has subtly, but steadily, sought to change international law with regard to certain unilateral uses of force. While it has not totally succeeded, it has accomplished enough to have made expectations of who and how the law is made and what the law *is* less certain than in the past."

This transformation is connected with the change that occurred in the nature of the UN General Assembly as many new nations were admitted. In the early days the assembly operated on the assumption that what was said there was based on international law or at least evidence of it. The new entrants were generally have-not nations and they wanted an international law that implemented their desires. The result is, as Reisman says, the inversion of many established rules about the use of force.

Though there was no judgment by the ICJ, much the same thing occurred when the United States invaded Grenada. In 1979 that newly independent, small island nation had its government overthrown by a revolutionary party. Events followed the same pattern as had happened in Cuba and, subsequently, in Nicaragua. Large numbers of political prisoners were held and the new regime engaged in rapid and heavy militarization with the assistance of arms and advisors from the Soviet Union, Cuba, and other Communist bloc nations. Grenada's neighbors, six Caribbean island nations, were alarmed, since Grenada's military force exceeded their combined forces and seemed to have no possible purpose other than the support of subversion to overthrow their democratic governments. A coup, probably the work of even more hard-line Marxist-Leninists, resulted in chaos, with no one group in control. Rioting, looting, demonstrations, shootings, and a round-the-clock curfew, enforced by threats to shoot on sight, left the island without a stable government. The other six island nations expressed serious concern, as did the United States, for there were about one thousand Americans on the island, many of whom were medical students. These Americans, cut off from the outside world, dependent on the People's Revolutionary Army for food and water, and confined to their quarters on pain of death, were effectively hostages. The State Department tried, without success, to arrange their release and evacuation.

At the request of other concerned nations, the United States invaded Grenada. When the fighting was over, a CBS News poll found that 91 per cent of Grenadans were glad the U.S. troops had come. Within less than two months, the U.S. armed forces left the island, order had been restored, American and Grenadan lives had undoubtedly been saved, and plans were under way for free elections. One would have thought that, outside the Communist bloc, the American action would have been joyfully received.

Not long after the invasion, however, the UN General Assembly voted to condemn the action as a violation of international law. The majority was even larger than the one that condemned the Soviet invasion of Afghanistan, an invasion that had none of the justifications the U.S. action in Grenada had. The vote had been taken, more-over, without even allowing the nations of the Organiza-tion of Eastern Caribbean States or the United States to present their case. Yet once more many American inter-national law professors responded according to their political views. Nine professors signed an article stating that the United States was "in egregious violation of international law" and that the lack of the "imprimatur" of the Organization of the American States would "raise serious doubts concerning the international legitimacy of any successor government." That reaction was so incredible that it comes close to calling into question the professors' grip on reality. Apparently, a Communist dictatorship installed by violence was internationally legitimate, while a successor government chosen democratically by the people of Grenada was not.

There is nothing here that deserves to be called "law" in any sense. The *American Journal of International Law* ran separate symposia of the Grenadan invasion and American support of the Nicaraguan contras. The various experts took almost every position imaginable, from the assertion that the United States is a dangerous international outlaw to the contention that everything done exemplified devotion to the rule of law. The arguments in defense of the United States's actions seemed to me far more persuasive than those condemning those actions, but I quickly realized that I was judging not on grounds that might be called legal but on political and moral considerations. I have no doubt that others, on both sides, did the same. The "law" itself seemed infinitely flexible and indeterminate.

Senator Daniel Patrick Moynihan, an international law enthusiast (he's on record for saying, "International law *exists*. It is not an option. It is a fact"), has stated a contradiction that lies at the heart of international law and accounts for its indeterminacy:

> An ancient doctrine (going back at least to Grotius) is *rebus sic stantibus*, which denotes "a tacit condition, said to attach to all treaties, that they shall cease to be obligatory as soon as the state of facts and conditions upon which they were

founded has substantially changed" (*Black's Law Dictionary*). For all that Chapter II of the charter of the Organization of the American States requires of members "the effective exercise of representative democracy," this is not going to be the political norm of this hemisphere or this world during the foreseeable future. It had once looked that way; it no longer does. Circumstances have changed. What has not changed – what the United States must strive to make clear has not changed – is the first rule of international law: *Pacta sunt servanda*, agreements must be kept.

But if the condition on which the United States agreed to the OAS Charter – that the members would be democracies – has changed, why does not *rebus sic stantibus* relieve us of the obligation to keep the rest of the agreement? It is one thing to contract with democracies and quite another to be bound when the parties become totalitarian or authoritarian. Moynihan's argument, and his condemnation of America's action in Grenada, lack coherence.

The crusade to lodge control of the employment of armed force in international bodies continues. As John Bolton, who has since become undersecretary of state for arms control and international security, put it:

During the NATO air war against Yugoslavia, Secretary General Kofi Annan expressed the predominant view that "unless the Security Council is restored to its pre-eminent position as the sole source of legitimacy on the use of force, we are on a dangerous path to anarchy." Shortly thereafter, in a report to the United Nations' membership, Annan repeated his argument, stating that military actions (such as the NATO air campaign) amounted to threats to the "very core of the international security system.... Only the Charter provides a universally legal basis for the use of force."...

UN High Commissioner for Human Rights, Mary Robinson, was even more pointed, announcing: "[C]ivilian casualties are human rights victims." She asked, "If it is not possible to ascertain whether civilian buses are on bridges, should those bridges be blown?" Her basic objection, however, was not to civilian casualties, but to the bombing itself. During the war, she said, "NATO remains the sole judge of what is or is not acceptable to bomb," and she did not mean it as a compliment. Even more basically, she, like Annan, asserted that NATO's lack of Security Council authorization violated international law.

Israel's Aharon Barak claimed the right to judge the deployment of Israeli troops in wartime. Annan and Robinson have gone one better. They claim the right of foreign nations (and, apparently, international courts) to judge the tactical behavior of United States troops in wartime.

No court of the United States would entertain a suit challenging the legality of U.S. actions with respect to Nicaragua, Grenada, Panama, or Kosovo. Various radical groups have tried to litigate American involvement in such operations, but were not successful. Our courts, under one legal rubric or another, essentially agree that there are inherently political disputes that are not fit for judicial resolution. As much could be said for all disputes about the use of force by one nation against another – but that is precisely the point about international law. The United States has not entrusted matters so gravely affecting its national interests, security, and foreign policy to American judges. Yet some will argue that the United States should entrust these issues to a court or a committee sitting on another continent, made up predominantly of jurists or members from foreign countries, and elected, often enough, by international bodies dominated on such concerns by nations hostile to the United States.

I once listened to a professor of international law defend the United States's actions in Grenada. The argument seemed tortured and artificial, and the most important considerations were omitted. When he was done, I asked whether three factors that most Americans deemed relevant to the matter counted in international law. First, the Grenadan government consisted of a minority that had seized control by violence and maintained it by terror. Second, it was a Marxist-Leninist regime and represented a further advance in this hemisphere of a power that threatened freedom and democracy throughout the world. Third, the people of Grenada were ecstatic at being relieved of tyranny and the ever present threat of violence. The expert replied, somewhat sadly, that these considerations had no weight in international law.

A moment's reflection makes it clear that, in the real world, they could not. In order to be international, rules about the use of force between nations must be acceptable to regimes that operate on different – often contradictory – moral premises. The rules themselves must not express a preference for freedom over tyranny or for elections over domestic violence as the means of coming to power. This moral equivalence is embodied in international charters. The charters must be neutral and the easiest neutral principle is "No force." The fact that this principle will be ignored by those who see international law as just one more instrument of foreign policy does not affect the matter.

But even the principle of neutrality is now being altered to the disadvantage of the United States and other democracies. The UN General Assembly has begun to redefine what it means by "the unlawful use of force": under the new system, those it regards as struggling for "freedom and independence" may legally attack their own government, and another nation may legally provide bases from which the attacks are launched – but it is illegal for the targeted state itself to attack those bases. This change operates primarily to the benefit of radical left or Muslim insurgencies supported by nations of the same outlook, and to the detriment of the United States and other democracies when they aid the nation under attack.

It might be said that we must accept moral equivalence in international law in order to have rules that are acceptable to hostile nations, in the hope that it will deter them from the use of armed force. Yet surely this argument about the power relations of nations is the same as preaching the rule of law to the Medellin cartel, in the expectation that, one day, the drug lords will be worn down by the rhetoric of idealism and submit to the law of Colombia. Even if we could hope that the aspiration of international law might eventually lessen the amount of aggression in the world, there is the present reality that it does not, and that it imposes costs disproportionately on liberal, democratic nations.

The major cost is that, by eliminating morality from its calculus, international law actually makes moral action appear immoral. It can hardly be doubted that, in the view of America and many Western democracies, it would be a moral act to help a people overthrow a dictatorship that had replaced a democratic government by force and to restore democracy and freedom to such people. Yet when our leaders act for such moral reasons, they are forced into contrived legal explanations. The implausibility of those explanations reverses the moral stance of the parties.

International law serves, both internationally and domestically, as a basis for a rhetoric of recrimination directed at the United States and other free nations. Those who disapprove of a government's actions on the merits, but who fear they may prove popular, can transform the dispute from one about substance to one about legality. The government can be painted as a lawbreaker and perhaps drawn into a legalistic defense of its actions. The effect is to raise doubts and lower democratic morale. Dictatorships have no such problem.

As currently defined, then, international law about the

use of force is not even a piety; it is a net loss for Western democracies. Senator Moynihan, speaking of international relations in Woodrow Wilson's time, said, approvingly, that "the idea of law persisted, even when it did not prevail." That is precisely the problem. Since international law does not prevail, the persistence of the idea that it exists can be pernicious. There can be no authentic rule of law among nations until they have a common political morality or are under a common sovereignty. A glance at the real world suggests we have a while to wait.

Since the action in Grenada and Nicaragua, the supposed international law on the use of armed force by one nation against another has become even more inconsistent and useless for purposes other than propaganda abroad and partisan wrangling at home. When the United States invaded Panama ("Operation Just Cause"), the Bush administration offered several legal justifications for the operation: defense of U.S. nationals, defense of the canal under the Canal Treaty, the need to apprehend General Manuel Noriega (who was charged with international drug dealing), and the need to support the democratically elected government. The international law journals tended to be critical of the invasion as a violation of law. Professor Louis Henkin thought it a "gross violation," while Professor Michael Reisman supported violations of national sovereignty where they were necessary to support popular sovereignty. Columnist Mona Charen contended that the United States should have argued the moral rather than the legal justification for the invasion, a position that accords with my own. Henkin himself, while stressing the crucial importance of international law, suggests how misleading it is to call that body of conflicting principles "law":

> Customary international law, and even the interpretation of a treaty, may also [like the common law] change in response to new needs or new insights. A state might knowingly deviate from what had been established law (or established interpretation of a treaty) in the hope of changing the law. But that state does so at its peril. It does so at the peril that it will not succeed in changing the law and will be adjudged to have violated the law. It does so at the peril that it may succeed in destroying or eroding established law, to its later deep regret.

It is difficult to see what "peril" is courted other than the peril that the United Nations will adopt a condemnatory resolution and that dissenters within the nation, including its professors of international law, will wage a verbal war against their country's action as lawless.

Professor John C. Yoo, noting the silence of international law scholars concerning NATO's actions in Kosovo, wrote that "the central defect in international legal scholarship" is that "[i]nternational legal scholars are only too happy to attack in very harsh language, wars with objectives they oppose." Wars to contain the spread of communism in Central America or to maintain the balance of power in the Middle East are denounced as violations of constitutional and international law. "Wars that promote goals long sought by international legal scholars, however, such as the advancement of universal human rights over the principle of state sovereignty, do not provoke criticism, because much of the American international law community agrees with the result." Moreover, "[w]hen the analysis of international legal scholarship becomes so result-oriented, it undermines the very nature of international law as law.... [It] serves to reinforce the idea that international law represents nothing more than the policy preferences and intellectual agendas of scholarly commentators, rather than neutral principles that govern the conduct of nations."

By contrast, there was little criticism of the Gulf War because President Bush obtained the approval of both the United Nations Security Council and Congress. While that tactic deflected criticism, it set what may reasonably be regarded as an unfortunate precedent. It is by no means a constitutional certainty that a president must receive advance approval from Congress before ordering armed attack, though it may be the prudent course in the domestic politics of the moment. The consent of the Security Council was obtained only because China abstained. In the future, the United States may not be so lucky. Fortunately, later events suggest that, if a precedent was set, it is a very weak one. United States participation in the NATO attack did not receive advance approval of Congress or the Security Council. Kosovo, along with other military actions around the world, weakens and probably erases the Gulf War precedent about the necessity of congressional or United Nations approval.

David Rivkin and Lee Casey summarize the rise of today's version of international law. Since the end of the Cold War, a number of international organizations, human rights activists, and states have worked to transform the traditional law of nations governing the relationship between states into something akin to an international regulatory code. This "new" international law purports to govern the relationship of citizens to their governments, affecting such domestic issues as environmental protection and the rights of children. Among other things, as the authors say, it would "nearly eliminate the unilateral use of military force; create the unattainable requirement of avoiding all civilian casualties in combat; promote the criminal prosecution of individual state officials by the courts of other states and international tribunals; and permit – or even require – international 'humanitarian' intervention in a state's internal affairs." International law poses a real threat to every nation's ability to make its domestic laws and to act abroad as its national interests dictate.

CONCLUSION

*The characteristic danger of great nations, like the
Romans and the English, which have a long history
of continuous creation, is that they may at last fail from
not comprehending the great institutions which they
have created.*

Walter Bagehot

One of the indispensable institutions of Western civilization is the rule of law. That rule is central to democratic government, a vigorous economy, and individual liberty. A functioning rule of law requires that law be understood to have force and moral weight of its own, a force and weight independent of the political and cultural struggles of the moment. That is another way of saying that the rule of law, when it is observed, is the guarantor of the supremacy of process in public affairs, and, further, that self-government, stability, and safety depend on that supremacy.

It is, therefore, ominous news that the rule of law has become confused with, indeed subverted by, the rule of judges. That confusion and subversion are precisely what judicial activism accomplishes. Activism in constitutional rulings can be employed in the service of any desired result; an honest reading of a constitution cannot be so employed. Activism enforces the objectives of a dominant minority above the democratic process. In our case that minority is the New Class, at least for the time being and for the foreseeable future, a group as authoritarian in its outlook as any other.

The old civics lessons were sound. Rule by the people, which all Western democracies proclaim, means that voters choose legislators and executives according to the policies the candidates offer, that those elected will enact rules, and that judges and juries will apply those rules impartially and as intended. Unless that pattern is at least roughly followed, public debate, elections, and legislative deliberations have little significance. Process comes first, substance follows.

The judiciaries of the West are by no means alone in flouting the rule of law. Jury nullification – the refusal of jurors to be bound by either law or evidence when the results do not fit their personal views – is increasing and, in America at least, there is even a national organization devoted to justifying and encouraging jury lawlessness. That group urges prospective jurors to lie about their views and their willingness to follow the law during the jury selection process. Lawlessness is also built into the bureaucracies that modern intrusive and ubiquitous government requires. Bureaucracies lay down most of the law that governs us with minimal accountability to either the people or their elected representatives and with minimal concern for consistency.

Perhaps a preference for immediate victories is part of the spirit of our times. No doubt to a large extent that is true. It seems unlikely that these developments could occur without public inertia and weariness with, even the active desire to abandon, the long-term safeguards and benefits of process for the short-time gratification of desires. That is always and everywhere the human temptation.

But it is precisely that temptation that a constitution and its judicial spokesmen are supposed to protect us against. Constitutions speak for permanent values, and judges are supposed to give those values voice. Instead, national and international judiciaries are, all too often and increasingly, exemplars of disrespect for the rule of law. Their example at the pinnacle of the legal system teaches a lesson of disrespect for process to all other actors in that system and to the public at large. A judiciary faithless to its duty teaches that winning outside the rules is legitimate and that political victory, in the legislature or in the courtroom, is the only virtue.

Both in itself and in the example it sets, judicial activism undermines the foundations of Western democracies. Born in Europe, central to the American and the

Canadian foundings, and fundamental to Western civilization, the ideal of the rule of law no longer commands much more than verbal allegiance. It has descended to the status of a phrase that judicial adversaries fling at one another. If we do not understand the worldwide corruption of the judicial function, we do not comprehend the full scope of the political revolution that is overtaking the West. The political revolution in Western nations is the gradual but unceasing replacement of government by elected officials with government by appointed judges. The areas of national life in Western nations now controlled by the judiciary were unthinkable not many years ago. What is now unthinkable may well become thinkable in the next half century.

The political revolution brings with it a cultural revolution. In reading the opinions of many judges, it is apparent that they view their mission as preserving civilization from a barbarian majority motivated by bigotry, racism, xenophobia, irrational sexual morality, the desire to oppress women, and the like. The New Class heartily dislikes bourgeois culture. Hence, courts everywhere displace traditional moralities with cultural socialism.

We are witnessing the growth of an international constitutional common law. It is international because national courts have begun to seek guidance from the decisions of the courts of other nations and because of the recent and rapid proliferation of international tribunals applying treaties, conventions, and what they choose to call customary international law. It is constitutional in that courts insist that their rulings control legislatures and that the legislatures obey. It is common law because the courts piece together, case by case, a fabric of law composed of New Class virtues. This new international constitutional common law is illegitimate in each of its aspects.

Internationalism is illegitimate when courts decide to interpret their own constitutions with guidance from the decisions of foreign courts under their national constitutions. The American Constitution, for example, was framed and amended in the light of specific American history, culture, and aspirations. It has a meaning given to it not only by judicial decisions but by the practices of national and state governments. Why an American court should take guidance from the decisions of the courts of Jamaica, India, and Zimbabwe, reflecting the very different histories, cultures, aspirations, and practices of those countries, is not apparent. Nor is it apparent why the United States, Canada, the United Kingdom, or any other country should submit to the jurisdiction of international tribunals that will override the interests and desires of those nations.

Activism renders illegitimate the claim of this international law to be constitutional. We have seen activism at work in the United States, Canada, Israel, Europe, and tribunals claiming worldwide jurisdiction. We submit to the authority of courts on the understanding that they are truly and accurately expressing the meaning of constitutions and treaties we have approved. When it becomes apparent, as it has over and over again, that the courts are not expressing the meaning of those documents but merely using the documents as launching pads for the reforms they prefer, the claim of constitutionality is revealed as fraudulent. So it is with much international law and its tribunals.

Finally, the common law aspect resides in the fact that courts everywhere are making up the rules by which we are governed, even as the early English judges made up English law before Parliament became the dominant maker of policy. The difference, of course, is that it shortly came to be understood that Parliament could change or abolish the rules the common law judges had created. There is no mandate to be found anywhere in democratic theory for judges to make irreversible major policies when elected legislatures are in business.

The problems created by activism are magnified as law seeps into the crannies of life. As Gertrude Himmelfarb has stated, "Today, in the absence of any firm sense of manners and morals, the law has become the only recognized authority. Just as the state often acts as a surrogate for the dysfunctional family, so the law is the surrogate for a dysfunctional culture and ethos." One might add that the law invented by judges is a major cause of the dysfunction that it then undertakes to cure. "To all the other 'diseases of democracy,'" she continues, "we may now add the mania for litigation. As the law has become more intrusive, so has the judiciary.... The law, we are discovering, is too serious a matter to be left to lawyers or even judges." Our dilemma is that we have so far found no way to retrieve constitutional law from the exclusive control of judges and to restore it to democratic legitimacy. Such action would require that judges conform their rule to principles actually found within the constitutions they apply and, in turn, practice republican virtue. As Himmelfarb says, "Republican government means self-government – self-discipline, self-restraint, self-control, self-reliance – 'republican virtue,' in short." Judicial coercion of New Class virtue is the antithesis of republican virtue.

The liberal mindset refuses to recognize that real institutions can never even approximate ideal institutions. The pursuit of the ideal necessarily teaches an abstract, universalistic style of reasoning and legal argument. It leads to an incessant harping on rights ("rights talk," as Mary Ann Glendon calls it) that impoverishes political and legal discourse, but it inflicts more damage than that. Rights become weapons in political, cultural, and legal struggles for moral superiority accompanied, of course, by the redistribution, in the claimants' favor, of wealth and privilege. The advantages of special rights are obvious, and so the claims of rights proliferate. Given the power of rights rhetoric, there is no easy defense or resistance. The result is a clamorous public square, with groups pitted against one another and the consequent deterioration of the community's fabric. One outcome is the further politicization of law, as courts decide which groups are to receive the rights and which must surrender portions of theirs. In that process, nothing resembling a rule of law can be discerned.

Universalistic rhetoric, which is what rights talk is, teaches disrespect for the actual institutions of any nation, perhaps particularly democratic nations. The institutions of such nations are designed to allow compromise, to slow change, to dilute and tame absolutisms. Such institutions embody inconsistencies that are, on balance, wholesome. They are designed, in short, to do things, albeit messily and democratically, that abstract generalizations about the just society bring into contempt. Abstract ideals can never be realized in practice, but the search for cosmic justice continues and drives courts on, carrying them away from the only task they are even tolerably fit to perform.

It may be that whenever the care of a constitution is given to judges, the outcomes described in this book are inevitable. Wherever there is judicial review, two forces are placed in opposition: the democratic principle of the elected branches of government and the anti-democratic principle of the judiciary. It seems not to have occurred to the designers of such arrangements that one or the other of these principles might in time gain ascendancy. But that is precisely what happened in the twentieth century, and the ascendent and aggressive principle is the anti-democratic one. The crucial question for all nations that desire to remain self-governing is how to tame and limit the anti-democratic aggressions of their judiciaries.

BIBLIOGRAPHY

INTRODUCTION

Elliot, Jonathan. *The Debates in the Several State Conventions on the Adoption of the Constitution* (2nd ed., vol. 3). Philadelphia: J.B. Lippincott Company, 1907.

Hutchins, Robert Maynard. *Great Books, The Foundation of a Liberal Education*. New York: Simon and Schuster, 1954.

Hayek, Friedrick A. "The Intellectuals and Socialism." 16 *U. Chi. L. Rev.* 417 (1949).

Chesterton, Gilbert K. *Heretics* (12th ed.). New York: John Lane Company, 1919.

Weber, Max. *The Sociology of Religion*. Boston: Beacon Press, 1963.

Kimball, Roger. *The Long March: How the Cultural Revolution of the 1960s Changed America*. San Francisco: Encounter Books, 2000.

Berger, Peter. ed. *The Limits of Social Cohesion*. Boulder, Co.: Westview Press, 1998.

Minogue, Kenneth. "The escape from serfdom." *The Times Literary Supplement*, 14 January 2000, 11.

Lockhart, Kamisar, Choper, Shiffrin and Fallon, *Constitutional Rights and Liberties: Cases, Comments, Questions* (8th ed.). St. Paul, Minn.: West, 1996.

Levi, Edward H. *An Introduction to Legal Reasoning.* Chicago: University of Chicago Press, 1949.

Himmelfarb, Gertrude. *One Nation, Two Cultures.* New York: Knopf, 1999.

Devlin, Patrick. *The Enforcement of Morals.* London, New York: Oxford University Press, 1965.

CHAPTER 1
United States

Board of County Commissioner v. Umbehr, 518 U.S. 668, 711 (1996) (Scalia, J., dissenting).

Bork, Robert H. *The Tempting of America: The Political Seduction of the Law.* New York: The Free Press, 1990.

Kalven, Harry, Jr. *The Negro and the First Amendment.* Chicago: University of Chicago Press, 1966.

Bork, Robert H. "Neutral Principles and Some First Amendment Problems." 47 *Ind. L. J.* 1 (1971).

Neuhaus, Richard John. *The Naked Public Square: Religion and Democracy in America.* Grand Rapids, Mich.: W.B. Eerdmans Pub. Co., 1984.

Lasch, Christopher. *The Revolt of the Elites and the Betrayal of Democracy.* New York: W.W. Norton, 1995.

Ely, John H. *Democracy and Distrust: A Theory of Judicial Review.* Cambridge: Harvard University Press, 1980.

Speech by Justice William J. Brennan, Jr. to the Text and Teaching Symposium, Georgetown University, Washington, D.C. (12 October 1985), reprinted in *The Great Debate: Interpreting Our Written Constitution*, 11 (The Federalist Society 1986).

Morton, F.L. and Rainer Knopff. *The Charter Revolution and the Court Party.* Peterborough, Ont.: Broadview Press, 2000.

Troy, Daniel E. "Bar Brawl, The ABA prepares to fight dirty." *National Review*, 23 November 1998, 28.

Chapter 2
Canada

Manfredi, Christopher. *Judicial Power and the Charter: Canada and the Paradox of Liberal Constitutionalism* (2d ed.). Toronto, Ont.; Oxford; New York: Oxford University Press, 2001.

Justice Claire L'Heureux-Dubé. Notes for her opening remarks to the panel discussion: "Same-Sex Partnerships in Canada." Conference on the Legal Recognition of Same-Sex Partnerships, London, 1 July 1999.

Morton, F.L. and Rainer Knopff. *The Charter Revolution and the Court Party.* Peterborough, Ont.: Broadview Press, 2000.

Knopff, Rainer and F.L. Morton. *Charter Politics.* Scarborough, Ont.: Nelson Canada, 1992.

Bickel, Alexander M. *The Morality of Consent.* New Haven: Yale University Press, 1975.

Southern Pacific Railroad Company v. Jensen, 244 U.S. 205, 221 (1917) (Holmes, J., dissenting).

Ollman v. Evans, 750 F2d 970, 995 (D.C. Cir. 1984) (Bork, J., concurring).

Chapter 3
Israel

Neuer, Hillel. "Aharon Barak's Revolution." *Azure* 3, Winter 1998.

Gordon, Evelyn. "The Supreme Court In Loco Parentis." *Azure* 10, Winter 2001.

Rosenblum, Jonathan. "The Man Who Would Be King." *The Jerusalem Post.* 26 September 1997, 7.

Tate, C. Neal and Torbjorn Vallinder, eds. *The Global Expansion of Judicial Power.* New York: New York University Press, 1995.

Haller, Mordechai. "The Court That Packed Itself." *Azure* 8, Autumn 1999.

Rosenblum, Jonathan. "The All Powerful A-G and Other Fallacies." *The Jerusalem Post*, 18 May 2001, 9B.

Gordon, Evelyn. "How the Government's Attorney Became Its General." *Azure* 4, Summer 1998.

Rosenblum, Jonathan. "Court Run Amok." *The Jerusalem Post*, 14 November 1997, 9.

Hazony, David. "From the Editors, The Year of Ruling Dangerously." *Azure* 10, Winter 2001.

Rosenblum, Jonathan. "An Enemy Everyone Can Hate." *The Jerusalem Post*. 24 April, 1998, 9.

Gordon, Evelyn. "Is it Legitimate to Criticize the Supreme Court?" *Azure* 3, Winter 1998.

Hazony, Yoram. *The Jewish State: The Struggle for Israel's Soul*. New York: Basic Books, 2000.

Bork, Robert H. "The Struggle Over the Role of the Court." *National Review*, 17 September 1982, 1137.

CHAPTER 4
The Internationalization of Law

Kissinger, Henry. *Does America Need a Foreign Policy?: Toward a Diplomacy for the 21st Century*. New York: Simon & Schuster, 2001. Copyright © 2001 by Henry A. Kissinger. Used by permission of Simon & Schuster.

Mauro, Tony. "Visiting Justices Get an Earful in London." *Legal Times,* 31 July 2000, 10.

Rabkin, Jeremy. *Why Sovereignty Matters*. Washington: The AEI Press, 1998.

Glaberson, William. "U.S. Courts Become Arbiters of Global Rights and Wrongs." *The New York Times*, 21 June 2001, 1.

Rivkin, David B. Jr. and Lee A. Casey. "The Rocky Shoals of International Law." *The National Interest*, Winter 2000/01, 35.

Krauthammer, Charles. "Milosevic in the Dock: At What Price?" *Time*, 9 July, 2001, 32.

Haberman, Clyde. "Israel is Wary of Long Reach in Rights Cases." *The New York Times*, 28 July 2001, A1.

Is a U.N. International Criminal Court in the U.S. National Interest? Hearing Before the Subcommittee on International Operations of the Committee on Foreign Relations, 105th Cong. (1998) (prepared statement of the Hon. John R. Bolton)

Goldsmith, Jack. "BOOK REVIEW: Sovereignty, International Relations Theory, and International Law: *Sovereignty: Organized Hypocrisy.*" 52 *Stan. L. Rev.* 959 (2000).

Boyle, et al., "International Lawlessness in Grenada." 78 *A. J. I. L.* 174 (1984).

Moynihan, Daniel P. *Loyalties.* New York: Harcourt Brace Jovanovich, 1984.

Bolton, John R. "Is There Really 'Law' in International Affairs?" 10 *Transnat'l L. & Contemp Probs.* 1 (2000).

Henkin, Louis. "The Invasion of Panama Under International Law: A Gross Violation." 29 *Colum. J. Transnat'l L.* 293 (1991).

Reisman, W. Michael. "Sovereignty and Human Rights in Contemporary International Law." 84 *A.J. I. L.* 866 (1990).

Charen, Mona. "Was the Panama invasion legal? That's the wrong question." *The Chicago Tribune,* 25 December, 1989, C19.

Yoo, John C. "The Dogs That Didn't Bark: Why Were International Legal Scholars MIA on Kosovo?" 1 *Chi. J. Int'l L.* 149 (2000).

CONCLUSION

Himmelfarb, Gertrude. *One Nation, Two Cultures.* New York: Knopf, 1999.

Glendon, Mary Ann. *Rights Talk: The Impoverishment of Political Discourse.* New York: The Free Press, 1991.